# THE
# RECRUITMENT
# BIBLE

# JOSH WELLMAN

First Printed in Great Britain by
Obex Publishing Ltd in 2020

1 2 4 6 8 10 9 7 5 3

Paperback ISBN:      978-1-913454-30-2
Hardback ISBN:       978-1-913454-37-1
eBook ISBN:          978-1-913454-31-9

A CIP catalogue record for this book is available
from the British Library

Obex Publishing Limited
Reg. No. **12169917**

# Table of Contents

# Introduction

In order to be a success at anything, it's important to understand the finer details.

The recruitment industry is a complicated beast and one which requires knowledge of every single aspect in order to succeed. If you want to source out the best clients, manage your database safely and effectively and select the right client for the right role, you need to have more than just a grasp on the subject. Of course, you also need to be competitive in the market - there are many agencies all vying for the same clients.

The role of a recruitment consultant is a varied one. This is a role that is unlikely to see two days the same. However, it is also a role that will bring immense personal satisfaction, when you select the right person for the role which will allow them to fulfill their personal potential. Of course, this also includes helping a business find the right staff to move them on to the next stage in their business growth plan.

The Recruitment Bible is going to walk you through all major aspects of the recruitment industry, covering 9 elements to complete your training. Each element has a variety of different content pieces attached to it, so whether you are aiming to start your own recruitment consultancy or you're beginning your career as a recruitment consultant within an established business, you can learn everything you need to know about this varied and demanding industry.

With aims outlined at the start of each element, you can track your progress and ensure your complete understanding, before moving on to the next element in the list.

Having a total understanding and overview of the role of a recruitment agency and individual consultant is a key part of being able to do your specific role to the best of your ability. That means taking the time to learn the basics, before moving onto the more specialised areas that will catapult your agency towards further success in the future.

# Chapter 1:

## An Introduction to Recruitment

**Chapter Aims:**

- To understand what a recruitment consultant/agency does
- To understand the general background to the recruitment industry within the UK
- Understanding the need to source out the right clients, not just any old clients

Understanding the complicated process of recruitment will unlock your understanding, but first, you need to have a true definition of what it is in the first place.

To simplify, recruitment is a process that allows you to find the best candidate for a specific role within a specific company, and to hire them to do the job. This covers a range of different tasks that make up the entire recruitment cycle, something which we will cover in greater detail later on in the book.

## 1.1 The UK's Recruitment Industry

Large businesses are in constant competition with one another and that means they need to find talented individuals to help them take their business to the next level. Recruitment can be a long-winded and costly process to go through, and if you have very little knowledge of the proper procedures, it can be a process that needs to be done again and again.

Businesses understand the need to save money wherever possible, but also to ensure that quality comes before anything else. For that reason, the recruitment industry is booming.

Businesses are outsourcing their recruitment needs to recruitment consultants and agencies up and down the country, hoping to reduce workload and have a better final outcome to any recruitment drive they do.

In the UK, there are countless recruitment agencies; some are small, some modest and others large, earning millions of pounds every year. You will find specialist agencies, those who specialise in finding specific types of individuals for businesses in a specific niche, or more generalized agencies. Whether you're reading this book because you're hoping to start up your own agency at some point or you've just been hired as a consultant within an existing agency, understanding the competition is a vital step if you want to succeed.

So, what does a recruitment consultant actually do?

Put simply, the recruitment consultant acts as the go-to between the prospective employee and the employer. So, you will be in the middle of the potential hire and the business who are hiring. You will work for both in essence - you have companies on your books who want to find the best talent to fill their positions and your responsibility is to help them do that. You will also have a responsibility to the individuals on your books, to help them find a role which suits their specific skills and to help them reach their potential.

This means that both benefit - the business gets the most talented individual for the job and the individual receives a step up on the way to their final career outcome. In order to tick both boxes however, you need to match individuals to roles very carefully indeed.

You can see how a recruitment consultant could easily lose clients - by matching the wrong individuals to the wrong roles, businesses are quickly going to lose patience with needing to go through more than one recruitment drive, and individuals are going to become annoyed that their time is being wasted.

As a recruitment consultant you therefore work for:

- Clients – the businesses you are trying to find employees for
- Candidates – the individuals you are trying to match a specific job. You will likely have a bank of CVs you keep on record to help you find the best match

The role of a recruitment consultant, therefore, includes finding clients and candidates, either via networking, marketing, or Internet searches, reviewing CVs, maintaining records in a way which meets data protection regulations, shortlisting prospective candidates for a role, interviewing candidates and communicating with the client to complete the hiring process.

This includes juggling several balls in the air at any one time; you need to communicate with both sides effectively and ensure that you keep on schedule, to avoid any untimely delays. Once hiring has been successful, you then need to ascertain starting dates and communicate these to the candidate, staying involved until the employment contract is finalised.

Within the UK, the recruitment industry is more active than it's ever been before. This is an industry that is worth billions and that means there are many agencies out there, vying for business and trying to outperform the rest. Recruitment is a very competitive agency and by entering into it, you need to be sure that you have the organisation and communication skills to overcome small issues that could turn into real deal-breakers for your business, or for your employer.

## 1.2 Why You Need to Find the Right Candidates

Understanding recruitment comes down to the basics, and that means that you need a solid understanding of why it's vital to find the right candidate for any specific role.

Sure, you could hire anyone and expect them to be trained up and develop on the job, but the chances of that match not working out are high. It's a far better option to be sure from the get-go that the person you choose has the skills, attitude, knowledge, and potential to be the right match all around.

The biggest asset of any business is not its goods, its services, its capital or its buildings, the business' biggest asset is its staff. Without high quality, dedicated and engaged employees, a business is bound to start failing pretty quickly. When employees aren't right for a business, they can start to affect morale within the rest of the workforce, which slows down productivity and starts to bring unwelcome conflict into the equation. All of this adds up to a pretty poor picture for the business and has a very negative effect on its chances for future success and growth.

By choosing the right employees, a business can grow, build, develop new ideas, and ensure that productivity is always at the right point. Productivity and profits have a direct link between them.

The right candidate should have:

- The right skills and experience
- Necessary qualifications
- A drive and determination which matches the business
- A shared vision
- Motivation
- Ethics
- The right type of personality for that specific business

As you can see, it doesn't always come down to what is on paper and that is why the role of a recruitment consultant is far more detailed than it looks. It's about understanding your candidates well and knowing where they may fit best.

Perhaps the reason why the UK recruitment industry is booming these days is that businesses alone are finding it harder and harder to hire the best employees for their needs. This comes down to:

- Not wanting to let go of long-term employees out of loyalty, even if they are no longer performing within their role
- A difficulty in finding the best employees within the locality of the business itself
- Managers often over-estimate their own skills and don't want to believe that an outside agency could do a better job in finding the right employees

The aim of the recruitment agency is to help a business see why employing the services of an agency is the best way forward.

## 1.3 Is A Recruitment Consultant the Answer?

Let's look at this from the point of view of a business for a second. This will help you to see why recruitment is such a vital tool for large scale businesses, looking for the best candidates for their available roles. When you understand this, you understand your role far more effectively.

Many businesses have recruitment departments within their organisation, but this hasn't stopped the recruitment industry from growing year upon year. This is all down to specialisation - a recruitment agency's business literally is recruitment! For that reason, agencies are still considered to be the single best way to find the best candidates, even though internal teams are evident in some places. Of course, the agency charges a fee for this service, but it often works out far less than having to constantly recruit for a position, due to finding the wrong candidate time and time again. You're basically paying for in-depth skills and knowledge.

What are the benefits of employing a recruitment consultant/agency as a business?

- **In-depth market knowledge** - Part of a recruitment consultant's role is to stay up to date with market news and as a result, that informs their decisions far more effectively. Consultants are able to give advice to businesses about the skills that are required for a specific role and any skills which may be required as a result of new technology or endeavours in that particular field. This ensures less chance to re-recruit in the near future.
- **Higher chance of success** - Recruitment consultants are trained to find the best candidate for the job which means that a company's staffing requirements are always going to be high quality and more accurate as a result. This boosts

productivity and gives the business a far higher chance of business growth and success.

- **A larger range of potential candidates** - Recruitment agencies have a large database of potential candidates on their books and that means a wider range of possible candidates for a job. As a result, businesses can benefit from specific skills and a smarter match. If you have a recruitment department within your business, you will not have access to the same pool of talent as an agency does.

- **A less time-consuming process** - A recruitment consultant handles everything, basically taking the entire process out of the hands of the business and freeing them up to go about their daily business. Recruitment can be time-consuming, and it can also cost a large amount of cash. By putting all of this in the hands of an agency, yes, you're paying money but you're probably saving money and certainly saving time.

- **International recruitment is easier when done through an agency** - Recruitment agencies are very useful for international candidate searches and can reduce some of the potential difficulties in recruiting from overseas. Again, this is all down to specialist skills and knowledge. An agency's whole existence is to ensure that a quality candidate is chosen for a role, meaning a higher quality result in the end.

Of course, there are benefits for the candidate too, not just the business.

When someone is looking for a job it can be an overwhelming process. Not all specific roles are advertised widely and that means you could be missing out on the ideal job, simply because you didn't know where to look. Working with a recruitment agency means that you'll be flagged up for any role in which your skills and experience match, therefore eliminating the worry of missing out.

Working with an agency as a candidate is also far easier because you have a tailor-made approach. You don't have to waste time searching through job after job; the agency will find the best ones for you and therefore save you the time. If you have a job at the moment and you're busy, that is an invaluable service to take advantage of.

Of course, part of the role of a recruitment consultant is to offer support to candidates, as well as offering advice on how to improve the chances of obtaining the desired type of role. When candidates pay an ongoing fee, they can access the services of a recruitment consultant over the long-term, therefore increasing the chances of finding that ideal and dream job.

# Chapter 2:

## Rules and Regulations Governing the Recruitment Industry

**Chapter Aims:**

- An understanding of the different regulations which govern the recruitment industry
- The importance of ethics
- The importance of a general code of conduct
- Knowledge of the different accredited bodies within the industry

Most industries have specifics that need to be adhered to, usually a large amount of red tape which would mean big trouble if the rules were not adhered to. The recruitment industry is no different.

As a recruitment agency or individual consultant, it's vital that you understand the rules and regulations which govern the industry, as well as knowing all about the ethics which come into play. This element is going to help you understand the specific regulations you need to adhere to, as well as the importance of ethics and a code of conduct to stick to at all times.

Due to the growing number of recruitment agencies around these days, there has been a need to implement standards to ensure that the level of service provided to businesses remains high and above all else, completely legitimate.

Regulations help to give protection to businesses, but it also protects the agency against any potential litigation efforts too. By ensuring that you comply with these regulations, you're covering all bases.

## 2.1 Understanding Codes of Conduct & Ethics

Every recruitment agency should have a set code of conduct that is given to each consultant and understood completely. Little like the mission statement of a business the code of conduct governs how all transactions are completed and to ensure that everything is ethical and done with complete fairness in mind.

The Employment Agencies Act 1973 is the main regulation that governs the recruitment industry, as well as the Conduct of Employment Agencies and Employment Businesses 2003.

Both of these regulations ensure that when sourcing candidates for jobs, the interests of the people involved, both clients and candidates, are placed well before any interest in profits. When the recruitment industry was first developed, there was more interest placed upon statistics, e.g. the number of placements, the number of successful transactions and a drive to hit these so-called targets often meant that the best interests of the people involved in the transactions were often put onto the back burner. All of that has now changed, with the implementation of the above two regulations and the need to ensure that every part of your business meets a specific code of conduct.

A code of conduct basically means that everything you do is ethical.

- All recruitment agencies should ensure that the practices they use help to boost the smooth running and the general standard of the recruitment industry within the UK
- Ensuring that all practices are transparent, honest, and carried out with thoroughness, diligence, and sensitivity
- Clients and candidates should both receive the same clear and solid advice
- All business must be conducted in a way which should not result in complaint or dispute

- Recruitment agencies should have a zero-discrimination policy and decisions should be made with fairness in mind

Put simply, when dealing with clients and candidates, you should ensure that you are fair and respectful at all times. There should never be a situation when profits or other means are put before the wellbeing of the people involved in your business. Any job opportunities or offer should be formed based upon experience, qualifications and a general fit of the candidate with the client, and not due to any other circumstances, such as race, gender, age, sexuality, etc.

## 2.2 Specific Regulations Governing the Recruitment Industry

Let's look into the specific regulations a little more deeply now and understand their specifics. We've mentioned the two big hitters, but there are a few others which have an impact upon the recruitment industry too, so it's worth knowing more about them.

---

## Employment Agency Act 1973

The Employment Agency Act 1973 was the first regulation that was passed to squarely govern the work of any employment agency. The sole aim is to ensure that work conducted by these agencies is done with the best interests of the client and candidates at heart. The main areas within this Act cover:

- A fee cannot be charged to British candidates unless that agency is covering careers in photography, entertainment or fashion. In that case, fees are allowed but must be appropriate and not inflated
- The Act allows fees to be charged to overseas candidates
- There are no restrictions on fees charged by agencies to clients, e.g. businesses looking for candidates to fill their available positions
- Personal information of candidates and clients must be kept confidential at all times and ensure that appropriate measures are followed to ensure that nobody is able to view such information, other than those who need it for their specific job roles
- Any information on the legal status of a candidate should be verified before being recorded and used as part of the recruitment process
- Qualifications should be verified before being documented and used in the recruitment process. This aims to stop false qualifications being placed on CVs and used in order to obtain a higher position than a candidate is realistically suitable for

- Any British national under the age of 18 cannot be recruited by a recruitment agency or consultant. However, there are certain loopholes in which an agency could receive written information from the parent or guardian in order for the candidate to obtain appropriate work
- Before signing a candidate, all information regarding a specific job role must be given, to avoid miscommunication and misunderstandings
- Records should be kept and maintained
- In any advertisement, a recruitment agency must make it clear that they are an agent, acting on behalf of a client, or they are an agency looking for candidates

It's also worth noting that a recruitment agency can be spot-checked at any time by an inspector, and if this occurs, the inspector is able to request information, documents, and ensure the correct running of the business.

## Conduct of Employment Agencies and Employment Business Regulations 2003

A more recent regulation is the above named, put into place in 2003.

This particular regulation is around ethics and ensures that clients and candidates are protected and dealt with in a fair and respectful way at all times. This ensures that discrimination is stamped out of the industry. There are however a few laws that are off-shoots of this particular regulation, including the Disability Discrimination Act 1995, Employment Equality Regulations 2003, Sex Discrimination Act 1975, and Race Relations Act 1995.

When delving deeper into the CEAEBR, you will understand more about how agencies should hire workers, both temporary and permanent. This should be done on the basis of skills, experience, and qualifications only.

## Asylum and Immigration Act 1996

This particular Act has an impact upon the recruitment industry when recruiting workers from overseas. It lays out the documentation which must be in place and the checks which need to be done.

This ensures that candidates are recruited correctly and fairly and that those who are recruited are able to work legally. Obviously, a recruitment agency who recruits a candidate to work illegally is going to face the full wrath of the law, along with financial penalties which can be substantial.

- Agencies must ensure that candidates are checked thoroughly in terms of documentation and that all documentation is legitimate
- Agencies who recruit overseas workers are solely responsible for checking a worker's legal status
- Copies of documentation must be kept on record

## Data Protection Act 1998

The Data Protection Act is a huge subject and one which we are going to cover in more detail in a later element. For now, however, we simply need to point out that the Data Protection Act 1998 covers the storage and processing of personal data relating to the person. In this case, agencies must ensure that all information is handled sensitively, carefully and is stored in a safe and confidential way.

Obviously, during the entire recruitment cycle, there is a lot of personal information obtained. This can include names, addresses, date of birth, qualifications, employment history, religion, sexuality, etc. This information not only needs to be kept safe, but a candidate can ask to see any information kept on them at any time, via a written request. Candidates are also able to start legal proceedings under the Act against any agency that mistreats their information in any way.

This is by no means an exhaustive list of all the UK Acts which could impact the recruitment industry, but these are the main ones that will need to be kept in mind day to day. A high-quality recruitment agency, and indeed, a high-quality recruitment consultant, should remain up to date with any changes to UK legislation ahead of time and ensure that these changes are implemented with immediate effect.

## GDPR

GDPR is an EU-wide regulation. Post-Brexit this won't cover sole UK transactions but if you are recruiting international candidates, working with companies in EU countries or you're processing information from someone who is from an EU country, you will need to ensure that you're adhering to these guidelines. As a result, you should familiarise yourself very carefully indeed. Again, any company that fails to adhere to these guidelines will find themselves in deep trouble, with severe financial consequences.

GDPR has six principles, which are very similar to the older Data Protection Act, but which are slightly updated for the modern day. These include:

1. Lawful use, fair use, and transparent use of data
2. Limited only to the purpose for which the data is required
3. Minimising data, e.g. only holding the information you really need and nothing more
4. Ensuring data is accurate and up to date wherever necessary
5. Stored in a secure manner
6. Used only by those who need access and confidentiality is maintained

The overall rules of GDPR are quite lengthy, so it is important that as the owner of a recruitment company you know the summarised responsibilities you hold and you adhere to them at all times. The main points to remember are:

- GDPR allows individuals and companies to know what information is held about them and what it is being used for
- GDPR allows individuals and companies to know if their data is being shared with other companies or agencies
- GDPR allows individuals and companies to access the data you hold (as with the Data Protection Act) and transport it elsewhere if they choose – this is known as 'data portability'
- In some cases, GDPR allows individuals and companies to request that their data is permanently erased

- Certain companies are required to have a Data Protection Officer nominated within their workforce, who is responsible for handling requests to view data and any other issues related to the Act. This person is also responsible for ensuring that GDPR is implemented
- GDPR states that companies who experience data breaches must inform those affected within 72 hours of the breach occurring

The reason this is all so pertinent to you as a recruitment company is because you are going to hold a lot of relevant information on your candidates and your clients. Regularly reviewing your records and destroying information that is no longer required should be something you do on a regular and cyclical basis.

The consequences of breaking GDPR, in particular, are severe. In some cases, this can be a warning, if the breach is minor and it is the first offence. However, there can also be very large fines. The most serious breaches of GDPR rules can create a major headache for business owners, with fines that can go up to 20 million Euros, or 4% of the total revenue of that company. The GDPR fine will, therefore, opt for the highest of those two choices.

The information you hold as a recruitment company will not be manual. Gone are the days when you had paper-based records and held them in a filing cabinet. If you choose to go down that route, you're seriously outdated and need to understand how technology runs the recruitment world. You need to hold data securely, and a Customer Relationship Management (CRM) system is the best way to do this! CRM systems also help speed up your day to day functions, help you stay more organized, and help keep track of your future employees. I strongly recommend looking into Vincere or Bullhorn.

## 2.3 Accredited Bodies Representing the Industry

Due to the fact that specific legislation and guidelines govern the UK's recruitment industry, that means there are also accredited bodies in existence too. These can be used to represent specific agencies and seek help and advice, so it's good to know about them and understand their specific aims.

Let's summarise them here.

## APSCo - Association of Professional Staffing Companies

Having been in existence since 1999, APSCo represents recruitment bodies in the UK and acts as an advisory service to the Government on legislation and specific guidelines that affect the industry.

By working with APSCo, this gives recruitment agencies a certain amount of credibility and also helps businesses to link together and network with others, creating a community of recruiters across the country. The vast experience of APSCo means that if an agency has any specific query or problem which they can't solve or they're not sure where to turn with, they can contact the body and they will have access to a wealth of specialised experience which could answer their query with ease.

Members will also receive a monthly report which gives information on recruitment trends across the country. This can help agencies to better target their client and candidates and inform placement decisions.

## AESC - Association of Executive Search and Leadership Consultants

Members of AESC are expected to follow a stringent code of conduct that focuses on high quality ethics. Having been around since 1959, AESC is an international body that helps to regulate recruitment in Asia, Europe, the UK and across America. The aim is to improve the practice and standards related to recruitment and to inform new changes to legislation which could take things to the next level for the industry itself.

AESC is a great option for any recruitment agency that does a large amount of international recruitment.

## REC - Recruitment and Employment Confederation

Having been around almost 100 years, REC is the longest standing accredited body in the UK and has a wealth of knowledge and experience members can tap into. There is, of course, a very in-depth code of ethics that members need to adhere to, and this is aimed at improving standards and ensuring that the industry benefits from new and innovative lines of thinking. These ideas are often put forth to political parties and help to inform debates which could help to bring, or update legislation and Acts related to the recruitment industry.

# Chapter 3:

## Standing Out from The Crowd

**Chapter Aims:**

- Understanding the importance of standing out as a recruitment agency
- Knowledge of the best strategies for selling your services to both clients and candidates
- Understanding the preferred supplier list and how to approach it
- Appreciation of the reasons why many recruiters lose out on business and how to stop it happening to you

As a recruitment agency, you are in direct competition with other agencies around the country. This is a fast-paced and highly competitive business and as a result, you need to ensure that your agency stands out above the rest. Understanding how to do this, whilst implementing the best sales strategies, will help the best talent sign with your agency. Then, as you get new clients on board, you can ensure that they receive the very best candidates for any roles they have available.

There are some very common pitfalls which many agencies fall foul of but understanding these ahead of time ensures that you don't fall into the same trap.

This particular element is packed full of information, and you may find it useful to jot main and salient points down as you move through it. Remember, however, you can always come back to any points you're not quite sure of or any points which you want to refresh your memory on at a later date.

## 3.1 How to Stand Out as a Recruiter

Every hour of the day, businesses are looking to hire the best talent for their available positions, and some are even on the lookout for the best talent to create positions for. Business is super-competitive and that means everyone is looking for the edge over those within the same industry as them.

Your recruitment business is no different.

The recruitment agency has never been more competitive than it is now and that means you need to do something different to the rest, whilst staying within the rules and regulations which govern the industry. If you need a recap on those, go back over 'element 2'.

Many businesses have internal recruitment departments or HR departments who handle recruitment in general. As we mentioned earlier, however, this doesn't always work and is never as effective as hiring a recruitment consultant to handle every aspect of the process. Businesses often miss out on great talent as a result of not having a wide enough pool of contacts or having slow internal departments that can't possibly move at the same pace as an agency.

Due to this competitive nature, recruitment agencies always have to be open to new selling techniques. That means selling your services as a recruiter to businesses (clients) and to recruit candidates to put forth for new openings. There are many different methods of selling and we'll go through some of the most effective strategies in a short while. The best-selling techniques ensure that a business can rely upon a recruitment agency to fill their requirements when it comes to staffing levels and quality.

The fact that there are countless recruitment agencies out there means you need to go above and beyond in order to stand out. How can you do that? And, what makes your agency stand out above all the others in the UK recruitment industry?

- **A deep candidate pool** - The more candidates you have in your pool, the more choice you will have when filling positions. Of course, that doesn't mean any old candidates and you need to be sure that your candidate pool is full of high quality, effective and experienced candidates. It's isn't about just numbers here, it's about quality. Having a deeper pool of quality candidates could help you to sell your services to clients and this may be enough to give you the edge over other agencies.

- **Extra services** - There are different services which an agency can provide to its clients. For instance, if your agency is able to offer temporary as well as permanent staff, and contract-based workers, this will give you an edge. Clients who are looking for workers for a short period of time may otherwise skim overusing your agency if you only offer permanent candidates. As a result, they will end up using a competitor's services and you lose out on business. In this case, it's about being flexible.

- **A swift service** - Without affecting quality, if your agency is able to fill vacancies in a short amount of time, you will have the edge over other agencies. There may be occasions when clients need to fill a position quickly and if you aren't able to do this, you may find that you lose out on business. However, if you offer a 'fast track' service, which still ensures high quality and the best candidates supplied, you will have a unique selling point which makes you stand out above the rest.

Anything you can offer which is a little different from the competition is going to give you the USP you need. However, you must be sure that quality and ethics are at the forefront of everything you do. It's no good offering a service if you're cutting corners in order to jump over the competition; in that case, you will lose business because clients and candidates simply aren't happy with your service. You also need to bear in mind that word of mouth advertising is still very strong, even in this day and age; with the advent of the Internet, more people will learn about what you do wrong than what you do well.

## 3.2 Selling Your Services to Clients and Candidates

To simplify things down, recruitment agencies basically sell potential employees to companies. On the flipside, they also sell companies to potential employers. It's a two-way service which benefits both, whilst allowing the agency to make a profit.

As with anything in business, it is a little more complicated than that. The recruitment industry is extremely diverse and there are areas of specialism that need to be covered if you want to have a USP which stands out above the other thousands of recruitment agencies in the UK. With that in mind, you need to employ a variety of different selling techniques in order to access the widest range of business for your agency.

If you want to convince clients and candidates to work with you, it's not always about focusing on the benefits of time and money saved. You need to highlight the other plus points too, including the other benefits that companies and clients can access.

As a recruitment consultant, you need to be very knowledgeable about what the client's business does and what they need. Only by doing that can you offer the best service and find the best candidates to fill specific posts. The consultant also needs to have a great amount of knowledge about the ethics and the mission statement of the company too. Remember, finding the right candidates isn't just about skills and experience, it's also about whether the person is right in terms of what they stand for and the importance they place upon ethics.

It's important to remember that business owners want to keep their costs low. This ensures that they can continue to make a profit and limit their overheads month after month. As a recruitment consultant trying to sell their services, you are responsible for kicking into touch the myth that recruitment services are expensive and unnecessary. You also need to highlight that using recruitment services can open up a range of untapped talent that would otherwise remain hidden from the client.

By understanding the specific businesses involved, the consultant can work out the best way to communicate with the owner, and therefore increase the chances of them agreeing to purchase recruitment services.

The basic selling techniques to use when trying to recruit clients and candidates alike are:

- **Showing evidence of your service quality** - This could include testimonials from previous happy customers, or you could ask companies to refer your services on, therefore showing that they were happy with your service and would use you again.
- **Ensuring that you are professional at all times** - Sometimes selling comes down to the basics and that means manners, professionalism and being approachable and friendly. When speaking to any potential client or candidate, ensure that you are warm but professional and that you answer any question they ask you. You should also give them ways to get in touch with you if they have any other questions, e.g. telephone, email, live chat. Also make sure that you answer queries in a timely manner via email, to avoid candidates or clients becoming annoyed and assuming that you're unprofessional. Small things such as this can make a huge difference.
- **Membership of accredited bodies** - Being a member of one of the accredited bodies we talked about in our last element gives extra credibility to

your service and gives your client or candidate a huge dose of peace of mind. REC is without a doubt the most credible and the most widely known, so it's a good idea to think about joining and ensuring that you inform potential clients and candidates of your membership. This can be done when calling, and it should certainly feature on your website and any literature you sent out.

- **Highlighting your USP** - Why should the client or candidate choose you over other agencies? You need to answer that question and show your USP in detail. Make your sales pitch a little different - clients and candidates have no doubt been contacted in the past by other agencies and if your pitch is the same as theirs, they're simply going to become bored and pass over your request. However, if you do something a little different, perhaps show videos or have an extra element to your sales pitch, you'll stand out and make the client or candidate think twice about passing over your services.

Before calling or generally contacting any client or candidate, sit down and think about the best way to approach it. Note down the points which will really hit home with this particular company or person, and make your selling pitch that little bit different, in order to be as unique as the person you're trying to contact. A generalised sales approach is easily passed over and forgotten, but creativity and uniqueness often stick in the mind and lead to a more successful outcome.

## 3.3 Taking Your Strategy to Another Level

Basic selling may not cut the mustard and you might need to move onto another level in order to secure extra business for your agency. Thankfully, the methods to do this aren't particularly difficult, but they do require you to think outside of the box and target your approach in a unique way, as we mentioned earlier.

A few tips to help you sell your recruitment services to a wider range and with a better success rate include:

- **Be honest at all times** - It's tempting to come up with huge promises and deliver a show-stopping pitch, but can you honour all the promises you make to the best quality? Whilst highlighting your USPs and impressing is important, it's vital that you're honest and authentic. Businesses and candidates can see through fakery a mile away and remember, they probably receive many calls just like yours. The best way to stand out and push your sales strategy to another level is to stick with good, old fashioned honesty. If something is going to take you two weeks to do, tell them that and explain why. By doing this, a business will feel they can rely upon you to get the job done to the best of your ability and they will use your services time and time again, whilst also recommending you.

- **Arm yourself with knowledge about their preferences** - This particular point is more important when targeting businesses, rather than individual clients. Before you reach out, find out as much as you can about the business in terms of their hiring preferences. A little earlier we mentioned knowing their mission statement and what they're about but you're going to waste your time and theirs if you contact without understanding what they need. Do they only hire those with degrees? Do they need temporary workers and you only provide permanent? Know what they need and target your approach appropriately, whilst ensuring that you can deliver on every promise you make.

- **Look for staffing demand trends** - A high quality recruitment consultant has their eye on developments and possible future demand. That means staying abreast of the news and reading industry literature. What business sectors are growing and may need a specific type of worker in the near future? By knowing this, you can make contact with those businesses and pitch what they may need for the coming months; you're also showing the business that you know what you're doing, and you have your finger on the pulse.

Again, this shows credibility and professionalism. You could also look into the particular types of skills which are in high demand in the area you're based. The more you know, the more professional and skilled you will appear to prospective businesses and candidates.

- **Time your calls correctly** - Calling at any old time isn't going to give you the best results. You need to be strategic to ensure that you reach the right person, at the right time. The first hour of the working day, before 9.30 am is a great time to reach out to new clients as, at this time, other agencies are often in team meetings or working out their call lists. This means you get in there first and therefore have a better chance of being chosen ahead of them. You should also make sure that you call more people than you plan to do, as it's possible that you won't manage to make contact with everyone you intend to call that day. By having an extra few as a backup, you reach your targets for that day and therefore have a potential amount of extra business at your beck and call.

- **Speak to the right person** - Make sure that you know the right person within the organisation to speak to. This means doing some research ahead of time and understanding who the key decision-makers are within that particular business.

Whether you specialise in a certain niche or not, the recruitment industry has three main groups who will often purchase your services. These are:

- **High volume companies** - This is a large company that will use your services time and time again for their staffing needs. This is the holy grail as it will bring you a large amount of cash revenue every single year. However, in order to attract these high-volume options, you will need to have a competitive pricing policy as they're likely to go for a lower cost, due to the amount of business they will send your way. It's important to weigh up the pros and cons of this, as new recruitment consultants may find that the costs aren't worth the effort, but as you build up your agency, these high volume companies can give you a regular income which allows you to try and sell your services further afield.

- **Highly specialised companies** - These are the types of companies that will require you to have a USP that calls out to their needs. They are also the companies who all recruitment agencies will be falling over themselves to sign up. The specialised services and products which these types of companies provide require highly specialised skills and experience too. Of course, these types of companies also earn more profits as a result of their specialisms and require high quality staff to cover their requirements. By selling your services to specialised companies you will be able to not only make a good profit for yourself, but you can also use this to try and sell your services to other companies in the same category. Offering specialised staff can be a huge USP boost.

- **Steady businesses** - These are the regular types of businesses that will give you a middle-of-the-road amount of business to cover your needs over the long-term. These fall in the middle of the high-volume businesses that need a constant supply of candidates and the specialised businesses that require highly specialised skills and experience. Businesses in this group can be any size, but the downside is that most of these types of businesses often have an in-house recruitment department. It is, therefore, your role as a recruitment consultant to persuade them why your agency can give them a higher quality service.

## 3.4 The Differences in Selling Recruitment Services to Candidates

So far, we have talked mostly about how to sell your recruitment services to clients and whilst much of the same advice also works for candidates, there are some subtle differences that you need to learn about. By understanding these, you can be sure that you're using the right approach and therefore signing up as many high-quality candidates to your agency books as possible.

Remember, a candidate doesn't pay your agency in order to find a job, but that doesn't mean that they're not an integral part of your work. Without candidates, you can't supply clients with workers, and the clients are the ones who pay the fee! As a result, you need to focus on signing up a pool of high quality, diverse and hard-working clients to help give you the best chance at providing clients with staff to suit their needs, and if possible, go above and beyond.

It's vital that you are open and honest about any employment opportunities with a candidate. You need to explain as much information as you possibly can and ensure that you do not withhold any information. You should also give information about the company, what they do, what they stand for, their values, and their history. This helps the candidate to decide whether or not they really want to go for this particular position and as a result, helps to motivate them too.

You should also ensure that the role is communicated to the candidate in as much information as possible. This also includes explaining why the role is vacant at the current time and what the candidate can stand to benefit from going for this particular opportunity. This could be the chance at getting a step on the career progression ladder within a large company, employment benefits or simply a good salary. You should also highlight any potential skill development which could come from going for this particular opportunity, but always ensure that you are honest and that you don't over-sell a position.

The candidate is likely to have questions about the role and the business as a whole. In that case, you should help to give them as much reassurance as possible, whilst always ensuring that you're honest. Take away their worries and concerns in the most unique way and they are more likely to feel that this opportunity is a good one for them.

Of course, you're always going to run into candidates who don't seem to want to make an effort to find better quality employment. Despite that, you should do your best to engage with these candidates to avoid them falling off your books and possibly ending up at the door of one of your competitors.

These are known as 'passive candidates' and the term also encompasses high talent individuals who are happy to stay in their current role and not attempt to make any in-roads towards bettering themselves. You can find passive candidates online, usually via platforms such as LinkedIn or by asking colleagues for potential names and then reaching out.

By having your finger on the pulse when it comes to potential rising talent that could benefit your agency, it's a good idea to reach out and keep in touch, in case the perfect role for them becomes available. When that happens, you can work your sales magic to convince them that this is a great opportunity for them.

## 3.5 Preferred Supplier Lists - What to do About Them

By selling your recruitment opportunities via cold calling, networking, emails and other means, you will come into contact with something called the PSL, or Preferred Supplier List. This is something you need to know about and understand and learn how to get around. If you don't do this, you will find yourself running into roadblocks when trying to sell your services time and time again.

When calling businesses in order to sell your services, many will tell you that they already have a PSL. This is an excuse in many ways but in some cases, it can be a truth. By telling you that they have a PSL, they're either telling you that they're not interested, in a polite way, or they're telling you that they can't hire you because they already have a list of places where they seek out their potential candidates for future jobs.

The PSL often comes in the list of a bank of CVs which the company has built up and review every time there is a potential job opening. However, no matter how many CVs a business has, they're always going to be interested in reviewing a high quality one.

In order to get around the PSL problem, you can offer to supply a client with a range of CVs free of charge. This is almost like the dangling carrot which will hopefully lead them to take you up on your offer.

Another way around this is to ask them about the suppliers they currently use and mention that your agency could be used as another choice, should there be an opportunity that doesn't fit with their current PSL. Remember, you are trying to sell your services and that means giving them an option - offering your agency's services as a way to enhance their current recruitment needs, rather than totally replace what they already have, is a good way forward and a great way to get around the issue of PSLs.

# Chapter 4:

## Understanding the Cycle of Recruitment

**Chapter Aims:**

- In-depth understanding of the cycle of recruitment
- Understanding why a careful process of requirement is vital for business
- How to handle clients in a professional way
- Understanding the shortlisting process of clients
- Learn how to manage paperwork in a safe and effective way

As we have already mentioned, you need to have a deep understanding of all the elements of the recruitment industry in order to do your job as a recruitment consultant well. That means knowing every aspect of the entire recruitment process, regardless of which stage of the process you enter, in your role as consultant.

Some businesses may like to have more input than others, and some may want you to begin your work at a different stage to others. Where you enter the process doesn't really matter, as long as you have a deep overview of the entire process in your mind.

This element is going to give you that overview, whilst also touching upon other important and related aspects, such as identifying the right strategy for each specific client you work with and how you should handle shortlisting and paperwork management.

## 4.1 The Vital Importance of a Standard Process of Recruitment

Whenever a job vacancy is advertised, there are normally many candidates for it. We live in an age which focuses on career advancement and when a high-profile business advertises for new staff, you can bet that their recruitment department will be inundated with applications. Sifting through these applications takes a large amount of time and if the business doesn't have a strong process in place, it's very easy to accidentally overlook the perfect candidate and therefore miss out on strong talent.

Receiving a large number of applications can also lead a business towards a hit and miss approach, in a rush to fill the position and continue productivity in whatever the vacancy is in. This approach is simply going to result in lost time over the long-term, as there will no doubt be a need to repeat the entire process sooner rather than later, as substandard staff is chosen in a rush.

Of course, the same advice works for a recruitment agency. You need to have a clear and transparent recruitment process that you follow for every single client. This standard approach ensures fairness across the board, and no business feels that they're being dealt with to a lesser quality than another on your books.

Having a standard process also means that the agency is more likely to identify the best candidate for the vacancy, ensuring that paperwork is completed and processed in a faster and more accurate manner.

Less time spent on searching for the wrong candidate saves time and money for both the agency and the client, whilst aiding candidates who are really suited to that particular vacancy.

As you will come to learn a little later in this element, the process of recruitment is a cycle that continues on. When the process is carefully planned and standardised, it shows professionalism and adds credibility to your brand. As a result, more clients and candidates are likely to use your services, compared to an agency who have a less organised process in place. Explaining this process can also be a good selling point when trying to obtain new clients and candidates.

## 4.2 The Recruitment Process Explained

As you will come to see, there are four main elements to the overall recruitment process. They are:

- **Step 1 - Acquisition of clients** - Identifying and pitching your services to clients and obtaining their go-ahead to work together
- **Step 2 - Strategy of recruitment** - Whilst following a standard recruitment process, consultants can tweak small details in order to find the best candidates for a specific vacancy
- **Step 3 - Attracting the right candidates** - This means identifying the right candidates for a specific role and pitching the vacancy to them
- **Step 4 - Management of interested candidates** - This part of the process covers application, short-listing, interviewing and final candidate selection

Within each stage, there are several different subsections and tasks which need to be undertaken in order to complete the process.

## Step 1 - Acquisition of Clients

The first step in the entire process is having clients with vacancies that you need to fill. Without this step, the rest of the process is totally null and void and not needed!

We've already covered many of the selling points to use when trying to find clients, and this step is basically about finding them and securing their business. You will then charge a fee for your services.

There are two levels in this first step. The first is finding and securing business with new clients you've never worked with before and the second is ensuring that the experience is positive and therefore ensuring that the working relationship continues into the future. The aim is, therefore, to keep the client on your books for the future.

Finding clients can be done via cold calling, meeting them in person, or sending tenders and different proposals to businesses that you feel could benefit from your services, as before, you need to do your research beforehand and ensure that your sales pitch is personalised and high quality.

Within this acquisition stage, however, it's a good idea for a recruitment consultant to develop positive relationships with all levels of the business, so the CEO, Managing Director, the line managers, etc. By doing this, you're showing that you can communicate at different levels throughout the business and you're able to identify the business' true needs as a result. This all adds to your quality of service and credibility as an agency.

As before however, we have covered sales pitches to potential clients in a previous element, so we won't repeat that content here. If you do need a recap, feel free to read back over the last element again, or for general reference.

## Step 2 - Strategy of Recruitment

The second step of the process means following a standardised procedure, e.g. the four steps we are talking about in turn, but also looking at unique ways and approaches you can use for each specific vacancy.

The whole point of a recruitment agency is to find the right candidate for each specific position, but it goes further than that if you want to stand out above the competition. It means looking at each client's needs and working on how you can best meet them. This is done via a strategy that is tweaked according to the client and the vacancy they are trying to fill.

Examples of a high-quality strategy include:

- Being an advisor for your clients and giving them ideas on the correct salary range for a role they are looking to advertise.
- Highlighting the agency's strengths and working to them, whilst also doing the same for the client and creating a strategy which encompasses both.
- Identifying potential pitfalls ahead and working out how to overcome them.
- Creating the right combination of searching and advertising for the right candidates.
- Evaluating each job role carefully and pulling it apart, in order to find the right person for the role.
- Adding in extra services which may enhance the recruitment process, such as online candidate assessments.
- Working with the media for specific advertising methods.
- Discussing with the client regarding not only salary but also employment perks which are expected for this type of role.

By developing an in-depth strategy and taking the time to do so before jumping into the whole process, you will find it far easier to find the right candidate and therefore fulfil their needs and the needs of the client. This should be your aim for every single client you work with.

## Step 3 - Attracting the Right Candidates

The next step is finding the right candidates for the job and selling the position to them. This is called candidate attraction and it is a vital part of the overall recruitment puzzle.

Remember, as an agency you are not charging a fee to candidates, but they are probably the most important part of the entire process. Without high quality candidates, and a large pool of them if at all possible, you will have no one to fill positions and clients will quickly realise that your promises were not credible, before moving on to one of your competitors instead.

You need to have a strong pool of candidates in your agency database and we're also going to talk a little later on about how to store those details, in line with data protection and other necessary guidelines.

In order to attract the best clients, you need to have a strong strategy in place which allows you to source CVs from high class talent and also be able to delve into pools of candidates who are less than willing to move forwards and reach out to you. These are the passive candidates we talked about in our last element.

A few methods to incorporate into your candidate attraction strategy include:

- Ensuring that your website is up to date and is delivering high numbers of traffic.
- Ensuring that prospective candidates see your agency as legitimate and credible; you, therefore, need to shine the best possible light upon your agency and allow candidates to see you as the best agency to work for, i.e. a leader in your field.
- Work with different media outlets to ensure that your advertising campaigns are targeted towards the right people.
- Create a strategy which ensures you not only look for the best talent for a specific vacancy but that you're also adding new candidate names to your database as you go along, therefore doing two jobs at once and saving time.
- Headhunting the best candidates using effective research, including networking and regularly searching using online methods. You can also use press advertisements to attract clients, as well as organising open days for prospective or interested clients to attend. From there, you can discuss possible openings with them and sign them up to your database. Remember, you need to be transparent and honest with candidates at all

times, including when you are looking to sign them up to your agency.
• Identifying passive candidates and enticing them to sign up to your database.

By having a strong pool of candidates within your database, you should have a list of names at your disposal for any vacancy that arises. This saves time but also ensures that you aren't constantly chasing your tail and trying to find workers whenever a vacancy comes your way via a client. As we have already explored, an agency that has a strong pool of talent is a huge USP and is extremely attractive to clients.

## Step 4 - Management of Interested Candidates

Once you have a list of candidates who are interested in the role, you need to work out how you're going to short-list them. This is something we're going to cover a little later in this element, so simply bear in mind now that it is part and parcel of the later stages of the recruitment process.

Once shortlisted, you then need to move onto the assessment part of the process. This usually involves inviting candidates for interviews, but it can also include asking them to prepare a presentation, using scenarios to see how they handle specific situations in the moment, IQ or psychometric tests. It all depends upon the type of role and the client's specific needs as to which you will opt for and this will be done upon discussion with the client.

After selecting the right candidate for the role, your task may be finished, or you may be asked to continue and help the client to prepare a letter of job appointment or even the contract of employment. Again, this will depend upon the needs of the individual client.

The process of appointing a candidate to a position is done by the client themselves, but sometimes the recruitment agency remains involved. It may be that extra checks need to be done, e.g. a medical or obtaining references from a previous employer. This is usually part of the recruiter's job role and you may remain involved until after these checks have been returned satisfactorily.

## 4.3 Managing Paperwork

During the recruitment process, a large amount of paperwork is generated. Some of this is electronic, but some of it is also paper based. A little later in the book, we are going to talk about why it is important to ensure that any information you keep on an individual is kept not only confidential and secure, but also that an individual can ask to see any information you are holding on them at any time. This is a hugely important aspect for all recruitment agencies to bear in mind as breaking any of the Data Protection Act guidelines could result in serious ramifications for the business.

As we live in a digitalised world, without a doubt the most common way to apply for a role these days is via an online application. As a recruiter, you will be responsible for collating these and shortlisting as a result. There are also CVs to bear in mind. Some clients prefer to ask for CVs and don't ask for an application form. There is no standard option here and it really comes down to how the client prefers to recruit.

By learning to manage the paperwork involved with job applications, you can ensure a more streamlined process and less chance of an incident happening, e.g. losing an important piece of paper.

So, why do some clients prefer CVs only and others want a full application form?

The plus point of just having a CV to submit is that a candidate is able to really highlight their personality, their achievements, and their qualifications in a way that reflects who they are. This allows you to get a deeper look into their inner psyche and determine whether they really are the best person for the role via their writing voice and how they have presented the document itself. Online application forms allow for very little personality and they are quite restrictive too.

However, the downside of CVs is that they are often long (two pages may not seem like much, but when you have several to read through, it can be time-consuming) and many candidates don't understand how to write the best CV to showcase their skills and experience.

Of course, online application forms are quicker and easier to process, but as before, they don't give the greatest scope for delving a little deeper into the possible best match for the job. However, online application forms are often considered to be the safest and most secure method, as these can be saved in Cloud storage and the client receives a confirmation that you have received the application, possibly cutting down on enquiries via the telephone or over email.

## 4.4 Shortlisting Suitable Candidates

The shortlisting procedure is a long and tedious one if not done correctly, however it is vitally important to get this step of the process correct. If you don't pay full attention when shortlisting, you could easily overlook the best candidate for the role, simply because they slipped through the net. The entire point of a client opting to use a recruitment agency is to ensure this doesn't happen!

There are two main points to the shortlisting process overall:

1. Looking at the CVs or application forms sent in by a candidate and shortlisting the best ones for the specific role
2. Whittling down your shortlist further by identifying the best candidates to invite for an interview or for testing, depending upon the role and your client's requirements.

Because shortlisting can be a long-winded task, here are a few tips to make it a little easier:

- Identify the number of shortlisted candidates you want and keep this in mind whilst looking through CVs and application forms.
- Identify the specific details that a candidate would need to possess in order to be considered suitable for the role, including qualifications, skills, and experience. It's also a good idea to think about 'desirable' traits which could help you to separate two candidates who are neck and neck on skills and experience.
- Pull out any CVs or application forms that do not fit the essential skills, experience, and qualifications. That should give you a lesser number to look through to start with. This could

also come down to any CVs which aren't clearly laid out or contain poor spelling and grammar.

- Look for any gaps in employment history or any candidates who move jobs a little too often. These are sometimes red flags, although not always. It's a good idea to look for explanations given in the body of text, but otherwise, this could be a reason not to shortlist the candidate. If you're not sure and you think the candidate could be otherwise suitable, you may wish to contact them to ascertain extra details.

- Before shortlisting, ensure that candidates have the legal right to work in the UK and have all relevant documentation, if required.

- Never be afraid to ask for input from a colleague if you're struggling to whittle down applications.

Once you have a shortlisted pile of CVs or application forms, it's time to move on to the next stage of the process, e.g. inviting candidates for interview or arranging any specific tests which need to be done prior to the interview.

# Chapter 5:

## Assessing Your Performance in the Recruitment Industry

**Chapter Aims:**

- Appreciate the competitive nature of the recruitment industry within the UK
- Understand what KPIs are and why they are important to recruitment agencies
- Understand the benefits of implementing and monitoring KPIs

A recruitment agency is the same as any business in many ways - the aim is; success, growth, profits, and a high-quality reputation which takes you further in the future. Without these things, you are going to be overtaken by your competition and end up with far fewer opportunities over the coming years.

It's hard to ascertain what success looks like, and although you might feel it, you do need a specific measurement of how you're doing in order to see whether any specific changes need to be made.

Businesses need to measure how they're doing, i.e. their overall performance, not only to work out what they're doing wrong and where they can improve, but also identify their strengths. As we have already mentioned in our previous elements, you will need to acquire clients in order to make your business work, and the identified strengths you see will form part of your sales pitch. If you can back these up with statistics and testimonials, even better.

There are many ways a business can look at their success levels, but one which is regularly used throughout many different industries is Key Performance Indicators, often referred to as KPIs. In this element, we will explore why KPIs are vital for recruitment agencies and the different types of KPIs you can look to use when measuring your own success.

## 5.1 Key Performance Indicators

KPIs are vital to help businesses measure performance. Not only that, but KPIs also delve a little deeper, giving you information on where you could improve. That information could then help you to overcome your competitors and drive your business further forwards.

Recruitment agencies spend a large amount of time communicating with different clients and candidates, whilst also networking to try and find extra opportunities for the future. The number of clients and candidates is a good KPI to go with, but that is only part of the story.

It's good practice for every single recruitment agency to have their own set of KPIs which they work towards and review on a regular basis. The information from the KPIs can then inform any changes that need to be made to ensure business success and growth in the future. One KPI which is certainly important for you to have is the number of successful placements over a certain amount of time, e.g. per quarter. This should be the bare basics of your KPI plan.

An agency that ignores the importance of KPIs means an agency that is far less informed and far less likely to thrive in this highly competitive industry. KPIs allow you to carefully check and analyse data and this can then help you to make stronger and more sensible decisions. However, it's vital that you choose the right KPIs; just choosing any old indicator is not going to see that you do very well and you need to think carefully about the right indicators you want to use to help you improve and better your performance in the future.

Taking the time to really identify the KPIs of use to you will prove to be an effective use of your time. You need to sit and think carefully about these and plan ahead. You should also know when you want to review your KPIs and what action you would plan to take as a result of the information they give to you periodically. Many agencies tend to focus on money, i.e. profits, or simply focus on the number of successful placements, but there are other useful KPIs to look into. We will talk in more detail about some of these later in this element.

However, it's equally as important to ensure that you don't have too many KPIs too. By having too many indicators to track and analyse, you're taking your focus away from what you're supposed to be doing, i.e. the professional service you are giving to your clients and candidates, and you're going to feel blocked as a result. By trying to hit targets all the time, you're taking yourself away from spontaneous decisions that could be a huge success for your business. So, in terms of KPIs, they're important, but having the right ones and the right number.

## 5.2 What Does Success Look Like?

There are major benefits in tracking your success, but you first need to know what success actually looks like! Does it always look like profits? Does it always look like the number of clients you have or the number of candidate details in your database?

Having effective KPIs in place will allow you to:

- Identify which areas of the industry or your work, in general, are affecting your success and how you can tweak details in order to improve your general quality of service.
- Identify the specific activities that need to be changed or improved to hit your goals.
- Use your time more effectively and plan ahead to ensure future growth.

These are the reasons why you should have KPIs, but in terms of what success looks like, that's harder to define. Everyone has a different idea of what success is to them. However, for a recruitment agency, success could mean a high income every year, increasing numbers of successful placements year upon year, the number of high-quality candidates in your database, traffic to conversation rates on your website, client testimonials, or market share.

How do KPIs fit into all of this? Because they give you the information that you would otherwise miss and by tracking them over time, you're not allowing a potential problem to build-up to the point where it becomes insurmountable. That is the mistake many businesses have made and as a result, many have failed.

In order for your KPIs to give you any solid information, there has to be groundwork in place to allow them to work effectively. This includes:

- Organisational policies and procedures which are already in place and being followed. Your KPIs would then inform you of how successful these policies and procedures are and whether any changes need to be made from an organisational point of view. Sometimes it's not what you're doing that's causing the issue, but the framework in place behind the scenes.
- Aims for each part of the business and its processes. This means breaking down the tasks you perform as a business and having specific aims in place for each. For instance, the number of candidates on your database at any one time, a target number of placements for each month, etc. It could also be about your mission statement, e.g. aiming to treat every new client with respect and honesty. Your KPIs will be able to delve into whether any problems arose as a result of not following that aim.
- Methods of measuring your KPIs already in place. For instance, how will you capture and collate information? Do you already have a database for your candidates, or do you need to design one? Do you have reports in place for profits or placements over the course of a month?

However, KPIs will only work if they give you the right information, e.g. statistics or data that is easy to analyse and not too excessive. You don't want to confuse matters here; you need this information to be clear so it can be acted upon accordingly.

To identify whether your business is performing well or not, perhaps you could sit down and ask yourself some searching questions, based upon the information you already have to hand.

- Is it possible for your agency to obtain more clients or candidates?
- Is it possible for your agency to obtain a higher quality of clients or candidates?
- Do your working practices allow you to do as much work as possible every day, or are there ways you could attempt to maximise this?
- Could your recruitment practices be improved in any way?
- Could you improve your conversation rates? This is the number of times you successfully get a candidate to add their details into your database for future vacancies

Acting upon these questions will certainly give you the best chance at obtaining success for your business.

Perhaps before deciding upon your own KPIs, something we're going to talk about in our next section, you should sit down and identify what success is to you. What does success mean for your business in your own mind? What does failure look like? Having these clearly defined will help you to create a set of KPIs that will prove useful for future analysis and improvement.

## 5.3 Creating Your Own KPIs

Creating a set of KPIs for your recruitment agency sounds like it should be a simple job, but in reality, it's actually quite difficult. You need to take the time to come up with a set of KPIs that are really going to work for you. If you rush the process and identify a set of indicators that don't give you the information you need, the whole endeavour will have been a waste of time.

In this element, we're going to talk about how you can look towards creating your own KPIs, but to give you a few ideas of options, the list below should give you some food for thought.

- Profits, both gross and net
- Per employee, lead generation and number of conversations
- Time taken to fill a vacancy
- Cost for every lead
- Customer lifetime amount/value

Again, these are just suggestions and may not be pertinent for your business. It could be that you want to focus your attention on a different area.

Once you've established a KPI, you need to give it time and not check it too often. However, KPIs are designed to be checked and analysed semi-regularly. You do however need to leave enough time between creation and analysis, as well as changes and analysis, in order to find out if you're obtaining enough information. You could check certain KPIs weekly, e.g. on a Friday afternoon or a Monday morning, but some need to be longer-term endeavours, e.g. checked every few weeks.

When you have your KPIs established, you need to ensure that everyone within the agency is aware of them and understands their importance. You should ensure that employees do not see KPIs as a way of checking up on them or watching them, and emphasise that this is simply an organisational tool towards betterment, and nothing to do with individual employee success within the agency. Getting this message across clearly will ensure that KPIs don't adversely affect morale.

The most effective KPIs tend to involve consideration from the following areas:

- **Profits** - The best KPIs lead you towards changes which will, therefore, bring greater revenue into your agency.
- **Benefits to the client/candidate** - The changes you make as a result of the KPI information will allow you to improve your service to clients and customers alike. This should also ensure that you attract new business via word of mouth referrals and testimonials.
- **Organisational procedures** - KPIs will inform changes to your internal procedures, the benefits of which are passed on to your clients and candidates.
- **Innovation** - KPIs could also allow you to explore innovative ideas that could bring greater success to the business.

## 5.4 Specific KPIs You Should Consider

You have free rein to create your own KPIs, however, there are some which recruitment agencies, in general, find very useful. Whilst you don't have to copy these, you should consider them carefully. To help you ensure the success of your agency and your own practice as an individual consultant, let's look at some specifics and explain why they work in the recruitment sector in particular.

### Time Taken to Fill a Vacancy

This is basically the time it takes you from a client notifying you of a vacancy or identifying a specific vacancy need for a client and then filling it, therefore completing the full cycle of recruitment. Whilst you shouldn't rush this process, it's important to ensure that you're not taking too long too. When you do take too long, clients are going to become antsy that they're not getting the candidates they need, and they're going to wonder why your service isn't as professional as you promised. In the future, this could lead them towards choosing a competitor over you.

A KPI in this area could help you to identify how long it is taking you currently and then work to make changes to your practices, therefore minimising the cycle time overall. It's worth noting however that some cycles will take longer than others, especially if many tests are required after shortlisting and particularly if there is a certain amount of specialism involved.

### Average Placement Cost

Obviously, a recruitment agency is a business at the end of the day. Although you are providing a service rather than selling a product, that also means that you need to make a sufficient enough profit to ensure you stay afloat and to ensure future business growth. Looking at the average cost of each placement will help you to see if your fees are fair or whether they need to be changed. It can also help you to work out whether your practices need to be streamlined in order to justify the amount of work you're putting in.

However, it's worth remembering that agencies do not charge candidates for their service, but they do charge the client. The fees which are involved in recruiting a candidate to a particular vacancy needs to be fair and competitive for both the client and the agency, from different posts of view. Obviously, you should at least breakeven but preferably make a profit.

**Placement Numbers**

This is a pretty easy KPI to use and one which will show you just how well you're doing, or otherwise. This is basically the number of vacancies filled over a specific period of time. Within this particular KPI, you can also measure potential placements.

This is placements which are in the pipeline, e.g. potential vacancies which are being discussed but which are not yet in the full swing of finding a candidate for them. This KPI can help you to look at how much business you might be expected to receive in the coming quarter or weeks ahead, and it will also allow you to assess how many vacancies actually come to fruition, e.g. how many are simply talked about versus how many actually translate to vacancies which need to be filled, therefore falling into the average placement KPI.

Looking at potential placements can also help you to work out your current workload, e.g. the number of recruitment cycles you're in the middle of but also the amount of advisory work you're doing as an agency, working between clients to look for new vacancies.

**Client Contact Time Ratio**

Evaluating the amount of time spent on the phone and trying to establish business from clients is a good KPI to use if you want to check that your individual consultants are putting forth enough effort to obtain business for the agency.

Spending too long the phone is often just as bad as not spending enough time if that call doesn't equate to a client signing on with the agency. By looking at these numbers, agencies can decide whether further training may be required or perhaps a different approach in general.

Overall, however, choosing the right KPIs is a matter for agency management, according to any specific needs or problems which are arising at any given time. A basic understanding of why KPIs are required and their benefits is a must-have for every single recruitment agency in the UK and beyond.

# Chapter 6:

## Attracting & Acquiring the Right Candidates

**Chapter Aims:**

- Understanding the meaning of quality candidate acquisition
- A deep understanding of what makes a high-quality candidate
- Learn how to overcome potential pitfalls when acquiring candidates for your database
- Learn how to create the perfect job advertisement
- Understand why brand identity helps you to attract high quality candidates

Whilst you do not charge a fee to your candidates, they are the most important part of the cycle. This is something we've mentioned before, but if you don't have high quality candidates who are going to fill the vacancies your clients have?

If you fill vacancies with poor quality candidates, your clients are going to become unhappy with your service and move elsewhere for their future recruitment needs. They're probably also going to make their dissatisfaction known to other businesses they may work closely with, and as a result, you'll lose out on potential business connections through them.

In this element, we're going to talk solely about candidates. We've covered client acquisition and we've talked at length about why you need to sell your services to clients in order to charge the fee to fill vacancies, but candidates are so important that they deserve a full element of their own.

## 6.1 Effective Candidate Acquisition Explained

The biggest asset your recruitment agency can have is a comprehensive and high-quality database, packed with information on the very best candidates in the country. That's the main aim of every single recruitment agency in the UK. However, to have that database, you need to put the effort in to finding those candidates and convincing them to sign up for your agency.

That means selling your services, as we talked about in our earlier element, and it also means ensuring that you keep all information up to date and secure. Again, we're going to talk about information and protection a little later on in more detail, such as its vital importance for recruitment agencies, and of course, businesses all over the country in general.

In order to succeed as a recruitment agency, you need to be able to provide your clients with the very best talent for their available vacancies. That means putting plenty of effort into candidate acquisition.

Candidate acquisition is simply a term for signing up candidates to your database and informing them of any specific job vacancies which you feel they would be particularly suited to.

Attracting candidates covers a wide range of different strategies, including networking, sourcing out candidates from online means, advertising for candidates who then directly contact you, networking on social media, referrals from other companies and even headhunting and cold calling. Using all methods is the best way to source out the best candidates for your database, and indeed for your clients in the end.

Successful candidate acquisition means that the candidate has submitted their CV to you willingly and this is then entered into your database for any upcoming job vacancies. It may be that you already have a specific vacancy in mind, and this is when you're more likely to use headhunting methods - when you know what a client wants, and you have identified a specific talent who would be perfect for it. We mentioned earlier about potential candidates or reluctant candidates. These are the candidates who aren't proactive in signing with your agency, but who may be persuaded if you call them and outline the specific job vacancy in greater detail. Remember, however, honesty and transparency are vital.

After you have obtained the candidate's CV, the acquisition side of the process is finished and can be ticked off. You then move on to managing the candidate, e.g. looking for the best position for them and informing them of the best vacancy for them, when it arises.

It's important to remember that you are not the only agency out there, and there are likely to be several other recruitment agencies contacting the best talent, trying to sign them up to their database. These days, candidates are very technologically minded; this means they're always online, using mobile and desktop technology to look for new opportunities. This means you need to be innovative and, on the ball, when it comes to trying to acquire them for your agency and avoid them from signing up with someone else.

When looking to match candidates and clients, you need to sell the vacancy to the candidate and ensure their interest and consent in applying. You can work to improve your outcomes in this regard by understanding the different factors which can affect the amount of interest you will have in a specific vacancy. They include:

- **The attractiveness of the vacancy** - in some cases, you will need to work harder to sell some vacancies than others, because they may not seem special or attractive on the surface but have hidden depths that need to be explained and explored together.
- **The job offer and what the candidate expects** - You may need to manage expectations or perhaps even discuss with the client in terms of the job offer a potential candidate could expect to receive. If the salary package isn't high enough compared to other similar roles in that particular industry niche, you will find that candidates are reluctant to put their interest forwards. In this case, speaking to the client and overcoming this problem is vital if you want to find the best talent for their specific vacancy.
- **How many other agencies the candidate is signed up to** - Remember, you do not charge a fee to the candidate, so they are free to sign with more than one agency if they wish. In this case, they may not prioritise your job vacancies over the vacancies and services another agency offers to them. This is where your KPIs from the last element will come in useful, so you can identify where you may be going wrong and where there

may be room for future improvement to overcome this issue.

## 6.2 Identifying the Right Candidates

To give you a thorough overview of the recruitment process in terms of acquiring and managing candidates, we now need to look at how you can find and identify the best candidates for your specific client.

Your client is relying upon you to find the best talent for their vacancy and that's a pretty hefty responsibility. As a result, you need to think in different ways and look at the problem from different perspectives.

Many recruiters find it useful to switch their perspective and look at the vacancy from the point of view of the candidate. What is it about this vacancy that is attractive and what part is off-putting? It's also important to realise that candidates know their worth these days.

Back in the early days of recruitment, candidates were the one's cold calling agencies, but these days it's the other way around. Candidates know that they are an asset and that they have the upper hand. With that in mind, you need to switch your perspective and see the situation through their eyes in order to not only identify but also persuade a client to apply for a vacancy that you believe they would be perfect for.

We mentioned in our section on shortlisting that CVs are a great way to learn a little more about the candidate in terms of their writing voice, how they lay out a document, their general level of spelling and grammar, etc. That is one way that you can use to ensure that you source out the best candidates for your clients. It often comes down to the smaller details, especially if you have two candidates who are similar in terms of experience, skills, and qualifications. By going the extra mile and putting forth a little extra effort, you will be able to source out a better end result for not only your client but also for the candidate too.

Again, always remember that candidates are the ones in control here. They do not have to sign with your agency solely, they are not paying you a fee, and they are the ones who can decide whether or not they want to put forth their effort towards a vacancy or not. As a result, your candidates can make or break your agency. That means choosing your candidates very carefully indeed and not rushing the process.

## 6.3 How to Attract the Right Candidates

By now you should be under no illusion just how important the process of acquiring candidates is. With that in mind, let's now turn our attention to how to actually attract and acquire them, rather than simply being general. Giving you the best advice here will help you to not only fill your database with candidate details but ensure that you have high quality candidates in there, not just general ones.

We've touched upon the fact that there are several different ways that you can reach out to potential candidates, but once you've done that you need to ensure that you sell your services in the right way. Again, always be honest. If you aren't transparent and honest you risk ruining the credibility of your agency, not only for now but in the future too.

You need to reach out and explain why you are the best agency for them, what you can offer them, your approach, why you are the most professional option and the types of clients that you currently have on your books. If you have a particular specialism, make sure you mention that too. If you have a particular vacancy in mind for that candidate, you could also open up about it, although do not mention specific company names at this point, in case the candidate decides not to work with your services and goes directly to the company instead. This doesn't happen often, but it's worthwhile to bear it in mind.

For the most part, however, agencies source out candidates before they have a general vacancy in mind. Then, they enter their details into their database and store their CV, until a potential employment opportunity arises. When it does, that particular candidate will be contacted by the agency and the vacancy will be explained, urging them to apply as you feel as a recruiter that they have the right skills, knowledge, and experience to be successful. Again, make no promises, however! They will be shortlisted if they have the best skills, knowledge, and experience against the other candidates who have also applied, there are no guarantees that they will be hired, and you shouldn't allude to that possibility either.

When you have a vacancy and you do not feel that you can fill it from the list of candidates you have in your database, that is when you would reach out to specific people you feel would be ideal for the position. You would do this if you felt that your database didn't contain the right person, it's the first time that you're attempting to hire to this type of position, or the candidates you feel are suitable within your database don't have an interest in applying for this particular position.

In that case, you would need to look externally and attempt to attract more candidates, not only to your database but to apply for the vacancy you have in mind.

Shortly, we're going to talk about how to create the perfect job advertisement, but for now, let's mention adverts as one way to attract potential candidates for a vacancy.

Adverts are more likely to be online these days, but we shouldn't forget printed versions, usually found in trade magazines or specialist industry literature. When you create an advert, you're basically targeting a specific group of people, i.e. those who have the necessary skills, qualifications, and experience for the vacancy you're trying to fill.

The problem with online adverts is that they can be seen by a huge variety of different people and in that case, you might be totally bombarded with applications that aren't up to scratch. As a result, you need to be as specific and targeted as you can possibly be. By doing this, you're more likely to find the people you're looking for, they won't get lost in the deluge, and you won't waste time sifting through CVs and applications which aren't to the standard you need.

However, job adverts can be very useful if the type of vacancy you're trying to fill isn't particularly specialised. This type of candidate acquisition and advertising can work very well for a new recruitment agency and it helps to boost your brand awareness and reputation within the sector and with individual job seekers.

Adverts can be posted on online job boards, via the TV or radio, on billboards, in industry or generalised magazines, via newspapers and websites, or possibly even posted through doors, especially via dorm rooms in universities, if that's the type of candidate pool you're aiming for.

Networking and cold calling, however, is a slightly different approach. In this case, you would need to have prior knowledge of a specific person and what they may be able to offer your agency. You will often find this information out via networking, word of mouth, etc., but it's important to remember that you cannot simply ask for someone's telephone number and then randomly call them. Social media is a far better approach and is more likely to yield the results you want.

LinkedIn is a great resource for high quality candidates within a specific niche and you can reach out and effectively headhunt candidates with ease from here. The fact that someone is on this platform and advertising their services means that they are probably looking to increase their skills or looking for new opportunities, which is a great way for you to start your email. From there, you can ask them to give you an appropriate time to call and discuss things further, if they are interested.

Before we move on to our next section however, it's important to remember that you need to obtain information on more than just skills, experience and qualifications. Of course, whether or not someone gets the job relies heavily upon these elements but it may also come down to other things, such as whether they're willing to travel, whether they feel they're a team player or they work better on their own, their technological skills and their general level of motivation.

When acquiring candidates, make sure that you ask as many of these types of questions as possible, and this information can be placed in your database, to help inform decisions about vacancies in the future.

## 6.4 How to Write the Perfect Advertisement

For the most part, advertisements will form the biggest part of your candidate acquisition plan and indeed, when looking to hire the best talent for specific vacancies you have with your clients. To attract the best candidates, you need to ensure that you write the best advert and post it in the right place.

Of course, we've already talked about where adverts may go, but what does the advert need to say and how can you ensure that your advert is the highest possible quality, therefore, reflecting positively on your recruitment agency and of course, on the client you're recruiting for?

Thankfully, much of it comes down to basics.

- **Ensure the layout of the advert is easy to read** - Make sure that you use headings and use bullet points to make information stand out.
- **Use language which is easy to understand** - Don't speak down to potential candidates, but make sure that you avoid using language which wouldn't be understood by someone who wasn't in a particular industry or business setting. This also means avoiding any abbreviations.
- **Keep your adverts professional by using a standard font, such as Arial or Times New Roman and make sure that the font is large enough to read** - Sometimes people are put off adverts when they find it difficult to actually read them! When you make it easier, the right candidate is far more likely to read to the end.
- **Mention where the job is based** - This needs to be clear. Sometimes the head office of the business stands out more than where the job is actually going to be located and it's often a totally different city in some cases. When you identify the location more clearly, you'll have fewer

applications to sort through; unclear location often means more applications from those who aren't actually suitable due to distance or unwillingness to travel once they find out where the job is actually going to be on a daily basis.

- **Avoid too much word count** - You need to mention all the specifics, but you shouldn't overload it. Stick to the main essentials, such as the job title, qualifications required, experience required, and of course, where the job is going to be located. If the salary is attractive, make sure you mention it. The advert is meant to grab attention and interest, leading to a candidate asking for more information via a job description, not to give all the information on the advert itself. Again, candidates may lose interest if there is too much word count or jargon involved, and that could mean you missing out on the perfect candidate for the job.

- **Do not make false promises** - Make sure that everything mentioned in the advert is based on fact. Do not mention anything which you can't deliver upon or which is not yet confirmed. By being honest and transparent, you're saving yourself a lot of hard work in the weeks to come, from disgruntled candidates and of course, associated clients.

- **Write in the first person** - Avoid writing in the third person as this can seem too impersonal. Instead, use 'you' because this indicates that you're speaking to that particular person and really pulling their interest in.

- **Avoid long paragraphs or blocks of text** - It's far better to stick to short sentences that grab the attention. Again, most people become bored very easily so if you have long rambling sentences, you're going to lose half of your audience before you get to the most important part.

- **Make sure that the advert reflects the client you're recruiting for** - If the client is a serious organisation, make the advert serious. If the client is a fun and creative organisation, make it a little more creative and perhaps even humorous, to reflect that.

- **Mention that you are a recruitment agency and enter your credentials, e.g. membership of accredited bodies** - This will show that you are credible and that the advert is equally as credible too.

- **Ensure that expectations are clear** - You need to make sure that the job expectations are very obvious on the advert, but whilst remaining within the short sentence rule. This will ensure that you have less unsuitable candidates submitting applications and making your shortlisting process far easier as a result.

- **Ensure the contact details are clear** - Make sure that you highlight and bolden the contact details at the end of the advert and give any instructions on how to submit a CV or application. The clearer you make this, the less calls you will have asking basic questions which could have been answered on the advert.

- **Use keywords for SEO** - Search Engine Optimisation is something you should be thinking about if you are posting your advert online. This means that your job advert will show higher up in the search engine rankings, therefore, increasing the chances of it being seen by the right types of candidates. SEO involves keyword research and then seamlessly inserting these keywords into your advert, in the most natural way.
- **Add media if possible** - If you have space, and especially when posting online, use media to help add value to the content and also to make it stand out. This means images and videos in particular. However, don't add these for the sake of it, make sure that they're relevant.
- **Ensure the first line is attention-grabbing** - Remember, adverts are meant to grab attention, so make sure that the very first line is interesting at the very least!

As you can see, creating a quality job advert is about capturing attention and not overloading potential candidates with details. There are some potential pitfalls you should avoid, including overloading the advert with too much colour and design - keep it simple and the details will speak for themselves.

## 6.5 Understanding EVP

The recruitment industry has several different abbreviated terms that all recruitment consultants need to understand in order to navigate their way successfully through the industry. One of the most important to learn is EVP.

EVP stands for Employer Value Proposition. This is basically the benefits and features that working with a specific company will bring to you. Every single business out there, i.e. every single potential client you could acquire, has a different EVP and you need to find the businesses with a higher EVP amount in order to obtain the greatest success.

How does this link in with candidates?

Because you need to understand the EVP of business accurately and completely, in order to sell your services to a candidate and encourage them to apply for a specific position. This helps you to communicate the advantages of choosing that particular vacancy, and therefore that particular business. The more you know about the business, the more knowledge you have about their EVP, and the better you can discuss a particular vacancy with a candidate who may be perfect for it.

Part and parcel of your strategy for candidate attraction should be understanding the EVP of every client in detail. When you create a job advert that covers all the bases and helps you to attract the right candidates, you can attract high caliber talent with EVP knowledge.

Of course, having a clear idea of the EVP of every client on your books is a time-consuming process, but it's one which must be done in order to improve the quality of your recruiting further down the line. Much of this can be done at the initial stage when acquiring clients and finding out their specific needs. You can research the client yourself and you can then ask searching questions to gain a greater overview of what they can offer candidates and the future career prospects for any candidate who may choose to work for that particular company. The EVP also covers benefits, such as a good quality pension scheme, salary, health care, etc. Any plus point goes towards boosting the EVP of that particular client.

In the past, when you've been looking for your own employment, you probably applied for more than one position at any specific time. The same will apply to other candidates in your database; that means that having knowledge of the EVP of every client you're working with can help you to attract the best candidates for that specific vacancy. The EVP therefore, gives the client a true overview of what it might be like to work for that client, rather than looking at all the positives.

A good candidate knows that no business is perfect, so an honest EVP will help them to decide whether the vacancy is for them, and therefore, avoid being hired for a job, only to quit a few months later. Obviously, this is a client's fear when it comes to recruiting new staff. Understanding EVPs can help you to avoid that pitfall.

## 6.6 Attracting Potential/Passive Candidates

A little earlier we talked about passive or potential candidates. These are candidates who aren't particularly active in the job market. They might not be enjoying the job role they have currently, and they will certainly be highly talented individuals, but they're not going to be the usual candidates that apply for jobs you put adverts out for.

However, these candidates are on your radar because you've heard about them or you've seen their profile on LinkedIn, for example. These candidates are high caliber and understanding a client's EVP is a key stage in attracting these types of individuals to your recruitment agency and therefore encouraging them to apply for a vacancy that you know they would be perfect for.

The problem with passive candidates is that they aren't motivated to search for employment. They're often content where they are, but they're not happy.

They simply go to work, get the job done and then go home, but you know they're capable of far more.

So, how can you attract these types of high-quality candidates?

The fact that a passive candidate is generally happy in their current employment means you need to really go to town on your sales pitch. You need to point out the major benefits of this type of candidate. This could include the fact that they may be ready for a new challenge in their life; sell the idea that whilst they're happy in their current role, perhaps everything is becoming a little dull without a new challenge to focus on. You should also highlight potential career progression opportunities, and the types of roles they may be able to work towards in the future.

Millennials, in particular, are very interested in achieving a quality home and work-life balance, that's another selling point you could use. If the client offers flexible working opportunities, use that as a USP and mention that there is the scope to possibly work remotely, work from home, etc. The more information you can give, the better. This will help the candidate to make the best possible decision for them.

You might think that mentioning the salary should be the first thing on the list, but potential candidates such as this aren't motivated by money; if that was the case, they would be more motivated to move around and find higher paid jobs. However, if a specific client is offering a very attractive salary package, you should certainly mention this, highlighting the other EVP points beforehand.

These types of candidates in many ways will help you to stand head and shoulders above the competition. When you have a high-quality candidate database, you're always going to make your clients happy. This ensures that your business thrives and that you continue to attract the best candidates and more clients along the way. At the end of the day, that ends up to growth and profits for your business.

## 6.7 Understanding the Market

When creating your job client profile, informing the development of your EVP for each specific client, you need to also do your homework in regard to the market for each specific niche.

If a client is offering a salary which is below the average for that particular market, that isn't going to help you to attract the best candidates. In that case, you will need to communicate with the client and help them to understand that their specific salary package is a little on the low side. Some businesses may be loathed to increase this, simply because they're trying to cut as many costs as possible, but it is your role as a recruiter to help them see that paying too low is going to reduce their chances of attracting the best talent for their business and future growth.

Benefits in line with the market average, and preferably above, will help to increase that particular client's EVP. This can then be passed on to the client and if the information is attractive enough to them, they will put their interest forward for the vacancy.

Understanding the market which your client is in means careful research. This is called understanding market position. Whether your client works with the market average or goes below it has a very real impact upon the quality of candidates they will find applying for their roles. However, this doesn't always have to be negative. Having a lower salary package than the market average means that you may attract lesser experienced candidates, but they are willing to learn and develop within the company. This can sometimes be a plus point for a client, as they may prefer to train up their employees to their own standards.

Discussing all preferences with your client beforehand will help you to ensure that you are all working to the market position and that you are offering real benefits to candidates. By doing this, your recruitment agency gains a reputation as being credible and professional and that will help you to continue attracting high quality candidates in the future.

## 6.8 Evaluating Your Candidate Attraction Strategy

Every so often, you need to evaluate your business strategies, to ensure that they're working to the best of their ability. In our last element, we talked at length about KPIs, however, there are some areas of your business which KPIs may not help with. In this case, you need to sit down perhaps on a three-monthly basis or so, and do some detective work, to find out if you need to make changes or not.

Evaluating your candidate attraction strategy is certainly something you should do semi-regularly. You won't be able to see much of a difference immediately, and that means you need to give it a few months before you sit down and really analyse the information you have to hand. Then, you can work out whether your current strategy is effective, or whether you need to change direction and focus your attention in other areas.

There are several ways you can analyse your candidate attraction strategy. These include:

- Analysing how long it takes you to attract candidates, i.e. from the first contact to signing up to your database
- Analysing the average cost of attracting a candidate
- Analysing where you find your candidates from, e.g. is social media more prevalent than networking?

Finding out where you find your majority of candidates is the easiest of the above analysis areas. All you need to do in this case is take the total number of applications you have received for vacancies over a set number of time and then group them into specific areas, e.g. sources. This includes social media, networking, word of mouth referrals, responses to general adverts, the candidates already on your database, etc.

From that, you will be able to see where you are receiving the most applications and therefore, where you are getting most of your candidates from. If you notice that you are only getting a very small number from social media, perhaps you should then focus your attention on developing your strategy in that regard - social media is extremely important these days and could turn out to be one of your biggest channels when it comes to attracting candidates. If this isn't working so well for you, changes probably need to be made in order to maximise your social media strategy.

It could also be that your agency has a lot of followers on social media, but you're not getting many conversions. You can find that information out by looking at your total number of platform followers, i.e. the number you have on Facebook, the number on Twitter, etc., and then dividing that specific number by the click-through followers. You need to do this for every platform in order to find out the ones which are working for you and the lower the number, the higher number of click-through followers.

Of course, you should also focus on ensuring that you always have one eye on increasing your market share. This means strengthening your brand in the recruitment industry and becoming more credible and more well known. Candidates are more likely to want to work with you if you're a highly regarded agency. It could also be that a candidate is looking to choose between you and another agency; if they have a stronger brand identity, they could opt for them instead of you because they assume, they are more professional and more reliable.

# Chapter 7:

## Managing Your Candidate List

**Chapter Aims:**

- Understanding what candidate management is and why effectiveness is important
- How to handle and screen incoming CVs from candidates
- How to choose the best CVs to take forward to the next stage in the recruitment process
- How to use an applicant tracking system
- The importance of customer relationship management
- Understanding Data Protection implications, including GDPR
- An understanding of background and other checks which may need to be performed

Once you have attracted candidates to your agency, you need to keep their details and their CVs safe. Of course, you also need to have an effective system in place which allows you to identify and pull out the best candidates for each vacancy.

Depending upon the number of candidates you have in your database, the methods you use to fulfill these criteria will vary. If you have a large number of candidates, you will need a database that has high quality functions to help you input criteria and receive results quickly.

Whilst how you attract candidates to your agency is vitally important, how you manage their details and communicate with them is equally as vital. Poor candidate management could mean that candidates choose to leave your agency and not work with you again. They will, therefore, take their talents to another agency and as a result, you're losing out on business and market share. They may also communicate their displeasure with your agency to those around them, therefore, meaning that you miss out on even more top talent as a result.

We have said it a few times already, but it's worthwhile reiterating this point - your candidates are your agency's biggest asset. If you don't handle them correctly, you're going to lose them and therefore lose your biggest asset. Without high quality candidates, you cannot fulfill the needs of your clients. In the end, that means your recruitment agency is going to fail.

# 7.1 The Basics of Candidate Management

Whilst there are many elements that attract a candidate to a particular recruitment agency, but they're far more likely to engage with you if you treat them with respect, kindness, understanding and if you communicate effectively on a regular basis. You also need to be approachable, i.e. the candidate should feel they are able to contact you with questions and that you will answer them in a timely manner, and you will help them in any way you can.

In many ways, a recruitment agency isn't just fulfilling a function, they're acting as an advisory service too. A candidate signs up with you because they feel that you are the best agency, or one of the best on their list, to help them reach their career progression goals and that you are committed to helping them find the ideal job vacancy for them.

Some agencies choose to take their candidate management strategy a little further and this is something you can consider if you have the time to do so. This could include help with writing a CV or resume, interview practice, and career matching, e.g. helping candidates to find out what type of role would suit their personality best.

As you can already see, candidate management covers a wide range of different functions and as a result, you need to be transparent and honest every step of the way, to ensure that candidates know you're working hard behind the scenes to find them their ideal job. However, it's important that you manage the expectations of your candidates too. This ensures that they are not aiming for job roles which they simply don't have the right skills for and that they aren't going to be going towards roles which are probably going to leave them disappointed after a short period of time.

Quality candidate management passes its benefits over to your clients, because happy candidates, with managed expectations and a clear vision of what they're aiming for, are more likely to stick with a job role once they attain it, and they're more likely to work hard to reach career progression opportunities that may come their way.

Whilst you don't need any specific skill to know how to handle people in this way, the instance you will develop after years of working in the recruitment industry will allow you to almost sense when a candidate is perfect for a specific role. This is something which will come to you with time and isn't going to head your way overnight! However, by working with the information you have to hand, e.g. as much information on your candidate as possible and talking to them about what they want to achieve, you will be able to achieve the same outcome.

Remember, any candidate could look good on a piece of paper, but not every candidate is the ideal person for every job. It's about finding the right fit and then talking to the candidate and encouraging them to apply for the position. If you assume that looking at CVs and working out who has the right skills, qualifications and experience is all that candidate management involves, you're missing the point. It also comes down to a general sense of whether that person is going to slot into that particular business and if they stand for the same types of values as the client itself.

In order to ensure that your candidate management methods are up to scratch, you need to ensure that several different factors are blended together:

- You have a quality USP which reaches out to the right types of candidates.
- You might decide to specialise in niche markets, in which case you will reduce the number of clients and candidates but perhaps be able to charge more. Or, you may choose to specialise in a different level of expertise, such as entry level or postgraduate.
- How you treat your candidates. It's vital that you treat your candidates as human beings and not just a number on a database. You also need to understand that every single person on your database is unique and that means they need a

different approach in terms of communication and also in how to get the best out of them.

- How talented you are at making your candidates feel confident in their own abilities. Without being false, you need to be able to help your candidates understand their own potential and how to reach it.

All of this blended together should help you find the right candidates for the right jobs and it will also ensure that you have happy clients at the end of the day. How to record all of this information and store it is something we will go on to talk about a little later in this element.

A good way to work out whether your candidate management strategy is working well or not is to look at the conversation rate between potential jobs and the number of candidates who choose to put an application in. The way you handle your candidates will show in how many applications you receive from them. If this is low, you may need to rethink how you're dealing with your candidates and look at what could be changed. Anything less than around 80% is considered nearing substandard level.

To sum up, candidate management is about communicating with your candidates, looking after their needs, offering extra services if necessary, collecting and storing information, managing their expectations, and preparing them for job roles that you feel they are perfect for.

Whilst clients are vitally important, most recruitment agencies spend more time communicating with candidates than clients. As a result, you need to be able to speak to your candidates in the right way. Remember, candidates know their worth these days, and they won't hesitate to move to another recruitment agency if you're not meeting their expectations.

## 7.2 Handling CVs

A high-quality recruitment agency is going to have a lot of CVs on their records and they're going to need to screen countless CVs throughout a working week. Whilst some may find this tedious, you should see it as a sign of success; the more CVs you're receiving and screening, the more in demand your agency is.

Part and parcel of the candidate management process is screening different CVs and working out which are perfect for a specific role and which aren't. Thankfully, you shouldn't have to do this by hand, or at least not the entire process, as technology has advanced to the point where it can help you to pull out the best candidates for a specific role, depending upon the criteria you input into the system. This basically means inputting keywords into your database and if those match with any of the CVs in your system, they will be pulled from the pile and presented to you for further analysis.

Is this a perfect solution?

No, but nothing is. It really does depend upon the right keywords being in the CVs that are in your system. However, these keywords do tend to be quite broad, so it's unlikely that you're going to have the best candidate for the job slipping through the net. It does, however, mean that you need to be cautious when choosing the keywords you want to input.

Having a selection of CVs flagged up however doesn't complete the process of screening. CVs are quite broad-ranging and don't go into the largest amount of detail. They are also written from the point of view of the candidate themselves and show only the basics, i.e. experience, qualifications, job history, etc. For a thorough overview of skills, the recruitment consultant needs to take a second look at the CVs which are presented to them by the system. This process is called 'screening'. Once this process is complete, you will move on to shortlisting and then interviewing.

Screening CVs can be a time-consuming process and you may find yourself stuck between several. In that case, it can come down to the basics in terms of

whether that particular candidate is shortlisted or
not.

When screening, be sure to look out for the
following points:

- Look at how the CV is laid out and presented. Is
  it professional? What does it say about the
  candidate? A CV which is neat and tidy, well
  organised and professional will stand out above
  the rest. A CV that is cluttered and difficult to
  read could mean that the candidate isn't
  particularly organised.
- Is the CV free of spelling mistakes and poor
  grammar? Sometimes the smallest details make a
  huge difference and if you are struggling to choose
  between two candidates and one has a CV which
  is littered with spelling mistakes and the other
  doesn't, that could be the deal-breaker. Poor
  grammar will be clear in how the CV reads; if you
  constantly have to go back over sentences and re-
  read, that's a sign that perhaps this candidate isn't
  the right one for the job.
- Does the CV contain the information you're
  looking for? A CV that is packed with information
  that is relevant for the role you're aiming to
  recruit to is a definite plus point. This means the
  candidate has everything you're looking for.
  However, it could be that the candidate has seen a
  job advert and basically tailored their CV towards
  that role to the point where they've ticked every

box on purpose. In that case, is it authentic? Or, have they looked at the job description and done everything they can to be selected? This is something you need to be on the lookout for and the more experienced you become in recruitment consultancy, the more obvious this will become. Obviously, these types of CVs can waste a lot of time, and you should focus on the CVs that focus more on the things they have achieved in their working life, and not on specific roles or responsibilities.

- Check the type of language which is included in the CV. If the CV is quite positive and focused on strength and creativity, it's a good match. However, if the general vibe of the CV is quite negative, that could be a sign that it's not the best fit. Standard lines or clichés should be avoided, and instead, look for strong and innovative language.

- Does the CV show their personality? Whilst a CV should always be professional, it should show the candidate for who they are in a professional role and should also show a little of their personality. That could shine through in their writing voice and style, so that is something to look out for and could give you a clue as to whether that particular candidate is right for this vacancy or not.

Of course, you should always base your screening process on what the vacancy requires, e.g. the right qualifications, a set number of years in a specific field (if applicable) and the right skills for the job, but you should also delve a little deeper. Does the CV show that the candidate has the same values as the client's business? Does it show that they are willing to learn or work on any skills which they might not have in their entirety on that particular CV? Does it show a passion for the role and motivation that will see them thrive in that particular business?

Remember that every recruitment agency has to abide by a code of practice and that means being ethical in every decision you make. When screening CVs, you're making the first important decision in a chain of other decisions to come. This has to be based on the right reasons and not due to any other discriminatory reason. Keep this at the forefront of your mind at all times.

When you're screening CVs, it's also useful to keep a copy of the job description and person specification close to you. When you're reading through various papers it's easy to lose sight of what you're really looking for, so by having those documents close to you, you can easily refer back and read back over what you need. That will refocus your mind and keep you on track.

It's also a good idea to write a quick list of the 'must-haves' you need for this particular vacancy and also have a general idea of the number of clients you want to shortlist after the screening process. Whilst you're not shortlisting at this stage (that comes next when you whittle the numbers down further), you do need to make sure that you're not choosing too many candidates that are simply going to be cast aside in the next stage, therefore, wasting time.

When you're noting down the skills and other elements you are looking for when screening CVs, you could give them an importance score. This will help you identify what you're looking for, bearing in mind that the information you're looking for could be in different sections of a CV - they're all different, after all.

It's good practice to place CVs into batches as you're sorting through them. These piles could be:

- **Top choices** - These CVs meet all the necessary skills and qualities.
- **Potential choices** - These CVs have most of the necessary skills and qualities but may lack some necessary details.
- **Not suitable** - These CVs aren't suitable for this particular vacancy as they don't meet the necessary skills and qualities to the right degree.

Potential choices may end up not making the cut in the shortlisting procedure, but they can be flagged up as possible top choices for other roles which are similar. As you screen the CVs, place them on the correct pile to save time at the end. You will then also be able to see quickly how many you have in the top choice pile from a glance.

There are a few common problems with CVs which could lead them to be rejected, other than poor layout and spelling/grammar. These include:

- **Gaps in employment which haven't been explained** - It's good practice for a candidate to explain a gap in their employment history, but if this hasn't been outlined, you may need to call them to find out why. It's possible that there is a perfectly good reason for this, e.g. the candidate was travelling and working overseas, they were looking after an ill relative, or they went back to school to retrain.
- **Regularly changing jobs** - Whilst experience is a good thing, a candidate who 'job hops' may be undesirable. This could mean that they have a short attention span, they have a problem with learning new things, or that they find it difficult to fit into established teams. Again, you may need to discuss with the client to find out why they have had several different roles within a short amount of time, but this is generally considered to be a negative aspect on a CV.

Once you have your top choices and potential choices, it's time to go through and shortlist those who you want to invite for an interview, or arrange any necessary tests or checks, according to the requirements of the client.

As you can see, screening CVs prior to the shortlisting process is time-consuming, but by keeping the job description and person specification close to you, you can ensure that your mind remains focused on the key skills and traits required for the job and stops you from deviating off course.

It's good practice to communicate with candidates who didn't make the cut, e.g. those who were unqualified for the role or whose CV was placed on the 'not suitable' pile. Not all agencies do this, but it will help you to stay in the good graces of your candidates if you have the courtesy to let them know when they haven't been shorted on this particular occasion and if possible, briefly explain why.

It's good practice to communicate with your clients by using their name and not a generic term, such as sir or madam, or 'dear candidate'. Ensure that your feedback doesn't focus on the negatives too much and ensure that you add a positive comment to any negative feedback you give. For example, instead of saying that they lacked the skills and qualifications for the job, you could say that on this occasion we felt that other candidates were more suited to this particular role, however, there are many other roles which you remain extremely suitable for and we will continue to do our best to find you the best match.

As you can see, you're giving a negative but adding in a positive to ensure that morale remains high. Not everyone takes criticism well.

When giving feedback and informing a candidate that they weren't successful, avoid too many words and get straight to the point. You should also do your best to give them notification of their not suitable status as quickly as possible, so they're not waiting around, and they can then look for other positions that they may be more suited towards. You can do this via the telephone if you want a more personal touch, or you can send out an email or letter. Obviously, in this digital age, email is the preferred option and is far faster than sending out a letter in the regular mail.

However, you should never give information to a candidate about the person who was selected for the role or those who were shortlisted. This is private and confidential information, even if you don't name names. Keep any feedback focused on the person concerned and not on those who were selected.

By taking care and time on the screening of CVs, you will save time further down the line, when timescales are shorter and big decisions need to be made. So, whilst screening may be time-consuming and difficult in some cases, ensuring that you focus your mind on the task at hand and select the best

CVs for the particular vacancy will ensure you have a better outcome in the end.

## 7.3 Using an Applicant Tracking System/Customer Relationship Management System

Depending upon the size of your agency and how you want to run it, you will need to have different systems in place to help you store information and pull it out when you need it. There are different systems you can choose from and larger agencies often have software companies design bespoke systems for them.

The most common type of system is an applicant tracking system and this helps you to record and keep track of the recruitment cycle for a particular vacancy. You may also see the term 'customer relationship management system'. This is basically the database in which you store your candidates' details and how you use it to pull out desirable CVs for a particular vacancy. For instance, we mentioned earlier about using keywords and asking the system to find CVs which match that criteria - you would do that via your customer relationship management system. This system would, therefore, contain all the information you need on a specific candidate, including their contact details, their CV, and any other pertinent information which you may use to help ascertain their suitability for a position.

Any type of system which contains personal information needs to be managed very carefully indeed. This is something we will discuss in greater detail shortly when we go on to talk about data protection and GDPR.

For now, however, let's talk specifically about applicant tracking systems as part of the recruitment cycle.

These days we have a host of different technological methods to use for any specific part of life, but when you're trying to keep track of a long-winded and sometimes complicated process such as recruitment, and occasionally severe cycles at any one time, a system which tracks and aids your work is always going to be useful.

The recruitment industry overall has become far more digitalised over the last few years, due to the large amount of information and data which needs to be recorded and stored at any one time. This is also useful for checking the effectiveness of strategies, as you can pull out data and reports from these types of systems, to give you information on anything which may need to be tweaked or changed for effectiveness and future success.

Of course, some people prefer to store information manually and work with it by hand, but that does have the downside of slowing down productivity. Let's look at why using an applicant tracking system might be the best option for your recruitment agency.

- You can handle a large number of CVs at any one time, without worrying about losing a document or not being able to lay your hands on it at a crucial time. Recruiters often receive hundreds of potential applicants for a specific vacancy and that's a lot of CVs to store and look through manually.
- Applicant tracking systems can help you to pull out the most suitable CVs for a specific post by using keywords. You would ask your candidates to fill out a screening questionnaire in some cases, which would be attached to their CV and therefore allow you to access keywords more effectively, without worrying about missing any top talent or any applicants falling through the net. For instance, let's say a client had specified that they want a prospective client to have five years of experience in sales. One of your screening questions could be "do you have a minimum of five years' experience in sales?" When your applicant tracking system is tracking through CVs to find those which fulfill your criteria, it would automatically pass by any CVs which answered 'no' to that particular screening question. You would

then be presented with CVs with the right amount of experience in the area you're looking for – in this case, that would be sales.

- This type of system is very useful for analytics. In that, you can analyse your strategies and find out statistics and numbers for what you're trying to drive towards. In some cases, applicant tracking systems can also serve as back up in the unlikely event of a litigation claim for discrimination. As we have already explored, the recruitment industry has a code of ethics that requires all agencies to select candidates on the basis of their skills, experience and qualifications and not to venture towards anything which could be considered discriminatory, such as sex, gender, sexuality, race, etc.

- There is less chance of an error when using a system such as this, and less chance of a top candidate to go missing or be left behind. It's very easy for this to happen when working with a manual system. When you have a lot of CVs to look through, it can be easy to lose one, miss one, or become tired and lose your focus. A system such as this cuts down on the chances of that happening. Of course, technology isn't foolproof, and as long as you regularly back up your data, you should have no issues with regard to lost information.

- Applicant tracking systems prove to be hugely timesaving. Again, manual screening and selection is a time-consuming process as it is, and if a system can save you time in terms of pulling out the appropriate CVs in your database, that's going to help you move the recruitment cycle on much faster, therefore helping your clients and candidates.

Of course, technology does sometimes have its limitations and if you're too rigid with your search criteria, you may find that it blocks candidates who would otherwise be a good match. The answer to this is to use broader keywords and search tools, and then weed out the candidates that it flags up from there. You could also consider using more keywords, which would then give you a larger selection. Yes, that does mean it will take a little more time to look thought these CVs and screen them, but it cuts down on the chances of you missing out on the ideal candidate.

## 7.4 The Importance of Data Protection & GDPR

As a recruiter, you need to have an in-depth knowledge of the Data Protection Act and you need to know the ins and outs of GDPR. These are guidelines you need to adhere to at all times, with no excuses and no questions asked. Failure to do so could land you in very hot water indeed. Not only would it severely damage the reputation and credibility of your agency, but it could lead towards criminal charges and a fine at best.

So, whilst you may wonder why we are discussing something which isn't about the ins and outs of recruiting, you should bear in mind that you have to weave these regulations and rules into your daily practice to avoid any adverse outcome. In this section, we will cover all of this in great detail and it's something you should make notes on if you need to. Be sure that you're clear on what you need to do and what you shouldn't do, and that you stick to it at all times.

The Data Protection Act 1998 is a piece of legislation passed by the UK Government which governs the information that companies hold on individuals. Within this Act, any client or candidate can ask to see what information you hold about them, and they would do this by writing to you and putting forth a request. You would then have to facilitate this in a timely manner.

In terms of how you hold information as a recruitment agency, you would, therefore, need to have a system in place which allows you to quickly pull up the information you hold on a particular individual and you should ensure that all of that information adheres to the 8 principles of the Data Protection Act. Those principles are that any information you hold on an individual should be:

1. Recorded in a fair and lawful way
2. Specific for only its purpose
3. Of an adequate amount only and only used for its specific reason
4. Always accurate and kept up to date at all times
5. Only kept for as long as necessary
6. Kept in a secure and safe manner
7. Never be transferred outside of the EEA
8. Stored and recorded in a way which takes into account the rights of the person involved

This basically means that any information you hold on clients and especially on candidates should always be up to date and accurate, that it should be recorded in an impartial manner, e.g. fair, and that it should only be used for the reason you have it; in the case of a recruitment agency, the information should only be used when screening an individual for a particular vacancy. The information should also only be kept for as long as it is needed, e.g. whilst the candidate is interested in working with the agency and it should be stored in a way that ensures its safety and security.

Again, an individual is within their rights to contact your agency and ask to see the information that you hold on them, and you have to facilitate this request under the Data Protection Act.

On top of this UK legislation, UK businesses also have to adhere to GDPR, which stands for General

Data Protection Regulation. This is an EU law which governs the protection and privacy of data across the EU and throughout the EEA. GDPR was implemented more recently, in 2018, and it takes into account digitalised information that we hold in this digital age.

As with the Data Protection Act, GDPR has a set of principles:

1. Information should be fair, lawful and transparent.
2. Information should only be used for its purpose and for nothing else.
3. Only information needed should be collected, therefore, minimising the amount of data that companies hold on individuals.
4. Information should be accurate at all times and up to date.
5. Information should be stored in a way which allows it to be easily identified and should only be kept for as long as it is required.
6. Information should be kept safe and secure at all times, protecting it against accidental loss or theft in particular.
7. Businesses hold accountability for any information they hold on individuals.

As you can see, GDPR is very similar to the Data Protection Act but has been updated to bring it in line with the digital age and expands past just the

UK, into the EU and EEA. This is particularly pertinent for any recruitment agencies that recruit overseas candidates.

All of this is very important for recruitment agencies to understand and adhere to. Recruiters hold a large amount of personal information on candidates, and to a lesser extent on clients too. At any given time, a client or candidate can contact your office and ask to see that information. That means you need to lay your hands on it quickly and it needs to not only be legible, but it also needs to be fair, contain no contentious statements or data, and it needs to be up to date at all times.

Ensuring information is up to date and accurate can be difficult if you have candidates on your database for multiple months. In that case, it's good practice to send out a questionnaire periodically and ask your candidates to highlight anything which has changed, e.g. their name, address, telephone number, etc. By doing that, you can be sure that you have kept all information accurate and up to date. You should also urge your candidates to contact you if they have anything they want to add to their CV, such as new qualifications or ongoing training they want to record.

The ramifications not adhering to both the Data Protection Act and the GDPR rules is severe. You may simply receive a written warning, but that in itself could instantly damage the reputation and credibility of your agency, causing clients and candidates to consider your agency unprofessional and unsafe. The more likely outcome is a written warning and a fine, and in some cases, depending upon how serious the breach, it could be huge; fines go up to 20 million Pounds or up to 4% of your revenue. That's a huge amount to lose for something which should be second nature to you anyway.

Due to all of this, the best way to approach data is as if it were a person.

## 7.5 How to Qualify a Candidate

We've talked about how to screen your CVs and we now know about the regulations that you need to adhere to in terms of keeping information secure. The next step in the recruitment cycle is to qualify the candidates you have screened as suitable for the role.

Qualifying is part of the client management strategy, and the entire aim is to work out whether or not a candidate is a good match to move forwards to the next stage in the process, for that particular vacancy. Of course, every single vacancy is different and every single candidate - a candidate might be totally unsuitable for one position, but a great match for another.

Qualifying comes after screening and is part and parcel of the shortlisting process. When qualifying candidates, you will separate them into two groups:

- REQ - Candidates who fit the requirements of the job
- SPEQ - Candidates who are in demand from your client but don't fit the brief that well

In this case, REQ stands for:

- Ready to Move
- Experienced
- Qualified

And, SPEQ stands for:

- Scarce skill
- Personality which fits in with what the client wants/culture of the business
- Experience which fits in with what the client wants
- Qualified

On paper, it looks like REQ candidates should always win through, but that's not always the case. Sometimes a SPEQ candidate shines and at interview, they prove to be the best person for the job. It's about having that instinct which allows you to avoid passing over a candidate who you simply have a feeling about, those who you know would work really well within that vacancy, but who perhaps lack a small detail or two.

Once you have your two piles of candidates, you can begin qualifying. This involves going through the CVs again but looking a little more deeply than before and searching for specifics. The following tips may help you to qualify your candidates to a high quality and therefore, choose the best talent to move towards the interview stage.

- Choose candidates who know what they want. By doing this you can be sure that they have realistic views of what to expect from the job. This means they're far less likely to second guess their decision and leave the business after a few weeks or months. This isn't what a client wants or needs and causes them to spend more money than they're happy with and lose time as a result. It also causes them to lose faith in you because your whole aim is to find the right staff for a business over the long-term.
- Is the client solely working with your agency or are they represented by several other recruitment agencies? Whilst this shouldn't be all you base your decision on, it does indicate that the client is serious about working with you and that they are serious about finding the right job.
- Are they serious about leaving their current job? Sometimes, candidates express interest in a role but when crunch time comes, they are reluctant

to leave behind their current job. This means you're wasting time and you're potentially passing over another candidate who would be a great match. Ensure that when you're searching for candidates, you assess their seriousness level or whether they're just 'testing the waters' of the job market for a later date.

- Have a number of shortlisted candidates in your mind and work towards it. However, if you're a little short of that number, don't force yourself to make it to your aim. It's better to have fewer candidates for interview, but knowing they're all high quality, than to have several who are high quality and a few who aren't that suitable but who are simply making up the numbers.

Once you have qualified your candidates, you will have your list to move on to the next stage in the recruitment process.

## 7.6 Understanding Skills Tests

Before the interview process begins, it's a common process to conduct skills tests. Of course, this really depends upon the type of role you're recruiting for but having a skill test aimed towards the role helps you to cut down on time-wasting and identify any qualified candidates who perhaps aren't as suitable for the job as they appear on paper.

From your shortlist of candidates, you would communicate with them and inform them of the need to undertake a specific skills test. This could be a scenario test, written or role played, it could be a basic Maths or English test, it could be a listening test, a group discussion, or it could be a leadership test. The list goes on, but it needs to be aimed towards the main element of the role you're recruiting for.

A good example here is if you were recruiting for a sales position. In this case, you could have a skills test which revolves around role-play scenarios. You would then get to see their sales techniques in person and work out whether they have the right approach, or indeed the right persuasion skills to get people to buy the products they would be selling, should they be successful in being recruited.

Skill tests help you to ensure that the candidates you're inviting for interview are going to perform well in the job and therefore cuts down on time wasted if they're selected and turn out to be less than high quality in practice. It goes without saying that you should inform the client of the types of skill tests you're thinking of conducting and ask them if there are any specifics they would like you to include. By doing this, yore tailoring the test to the specific needs of the role itself and that will give you a clearer idea of the suitability of the candidates you have in mind.

These preliminary tests are almost always conducted by the recruitment agency and not the client. From the results of the test, you would then move onto interviewing in person.

# Chapter 8:

## Understanding the Interview Process

**Chapter Aims:**

- Understanding the different types of interviews and how to choose the right one
- Understanding the different types of background checks and why they are important
- Planning interviews and ensuring that you cover all bases

The interview stage is an integral part of the recruitment process. By this stage, you already know who you think will be ideal for the job, but you need to test them out in person. At this stage, it's possible to be surprised by the outcome, no matter how long you have been working in recruitment. Some people are simply better performers when put on the spot, whilst others may find the nerves get the better of them and they may buckle under the pressure. It could be that the person who you have in your mind as perfect for the role falls into the latter group.

When interviewing candidates, it's important to remain impartial and not to have any bias towards any particular candidate. Again, you might think they look ideal on paper but in person, they may fail to shine. Whilst their CV has got them this far, the rest of the decision relies completely upon the interview and how they perform.

It's entirely possible that a CV has been written in a way that embellishes the person. This doesn't mean they have lied, but they may have written it in a way that makes them appear far more impressive in a certain niche than they are in person. This is why interviewing is so important, as it allows you to cancel out that possibility and identify the solid winner, the person who is 100% right for the role and therefore hired.

In some cases, there may need to be more than one interview with a specific candidate. This may be the case for managerial positions, when perhaps more than one interview is required with a one on one aspect and then a panel, or because you simply can't decide between two candidates and you need to finalise your decision by asking more searching questions. This is something you will decide upon beforehand, if the position is high profile, or you will decide upon after analysing interview results.

## 8.1 Different Interview Types and How to Use Them Effectively

There are several different types of interviews you can choose from, but the one you opt for will depend upon the specific role. Before we talk about those, however, let's solidify the importance of interviews in your mind.

- Interviews allow the recruiter a better chance to really analyse the candidate's skills in person, something which can't always be ascertained on paper.
- Interviews allow the recruiter a real-time glimpse into the personality of the candidate and from there they can ascertain whether they're the right fit in terms of fitting into an existing team, motivation, and their values.
- Interviews give the recruiter a chance to ask searching questions which link in with the responsibilities of the role. This is a good opportunity to use scenario questions, without moving towards role play, which isn't always appropriate or necessary.
- Interviews allow the recruiter a chance to clarify any points on the candidate's CV which they're not sure of. Ideally, this should have been clarified beforehand, with a quick telephone call, but this isn't always possible, and questions may only come to light further down the recruitment process line.

- Interviews allow the recruiter to really discuss the job role with the candidate in person and ascertain whether or not they are truly serious about it or not
- Interviews give a fair process as all candidates will be asked the same questions. This gives the best outcome in terms of choosing the right candidate for the role and ensures no discriminatory behaviour in terms of bias towards one candidate over the others.

It's also worth remembering that interviews are a two-way process and it may be that the candidate doesn't feel they want to proceed with the rest of the process if they're not treated in the right way at interview. It could also be that after you have discussed the role in more detail with them on a face to face basis, they decide it isn't for them. This is a good way to avoid time-wasting upon hiring, only for the candidate to decide that they've changed their mind. As we've mentioned before, this isn't something which a client wants to happen, and it reflects back on your agency very badly indeed.

The interview needs to be structured in a way that gets the best out of the candidate. This isn't a test and it isn't designed to trip the candidate up; it's designed to find out for sure whether they're a good fit or not.

According to the client's wishes and the type of job role being recruited for, there are different types of interview which may or may not be suitable. The main types of interview are:

- **One on one interviews** - The recruiter and the candidate are present, and the same series of questions are asked to each client.
- **Panel interviews** - The recruiter and perhaps two or three other professionals (often from the same agency but occasionally the client too) conduct the interview, asking a series of questions to the candidate.
- **Phone or video interviews** - It may be that the candidate isn't able to travel for a specific reason, or they may be away at the time of the interview. In that case, phone or video interviews are a common choice and can sometimes take the place of regular interviews in "normal" situations too.

Let's explore these in a bit more detail.

**Telephone Screening**

Telephone screening can either be done as a step in the recruitment process or it can be the proper interview. Again, this really depends upon the type of job you're recruiting for. However, the most common situation when you would use a phone interview would be to check out some information on the candidate's CV, and to check that it correlates with reality.

This would be done after screening the CVs and you would probably have flagged up a detail or two which you're not sure about, or something which just feels 'off' to you. Despite that, you feel the candidate has potential, so you don't want to count them out just yet. You would then contact them over the phone to complete the screening process, but this could also contribute towards the interview itself too.

Again, you could also use a phone interview if the candidate is unable to travel. Perhaps the candidate is away visiting family, they're at home sick, or they live away and it's difficult for them to travel back just for an interview. This helps you to avoid missing out on a potential talent, simply because they're not available to meet you in person. This type of interview should last around half an hour and you should schedule the call beforehand with your candidate, to ensure they have enough time spare and they're not going to be interrupted.

The downside is that you do not get to meet them in person and that means you can't watch for non-verbal cues, such as body language.

When conducting a phone interview, there is a general guideline you should follow. This is called the 5/20/5 method. You should spend the first 5 minutes discussing the job itself and the duties involved. You would then spend the next block of time (20 minutes) asking the interview questions, and the last 5 minutes should be for the candidate to ask you any specific questions they have.

Ensure that you write down your notes as you're talking. You could consider recording the call, but you would have to inform the candidate that this was happening beforehand and check they're happy to do that. Of course, you should ensure you conduct the call at a time when you're not going to be interrupted and that you devote your complete time and attention to it, just as you would a regular in-person interview.

**Face to Face Interviews**

The most common type of interview is a face to face interview, usually one on one although this can be done via a panel too.

Planning interviews beforehand will ensure that the entire process runs according to schedule and that you get the end result you're hoping for, e.g. to find the perfect candidate for the job and make a final decision.

It's important to meet with the rest of the panel, if you are conducting a panel interview, and discuss the questions you want to ask. Get input from everyone and come to a conclusion with a list of questions that are given to the panel beforehand and then kept with them on the day. Decide who is going to ask what question to avoid appearing unprofessional or unorganised during the interview itself.

Before the interview is over you should discuss with the candidate regarding when they can expect a decision to be made and how they will be informed if they are successful or otherwise. Never give any indication to the candidate at the end of the interview whether they have been successful or not; you may feel they have done well and have a great shot at being selected, but the next person to be interviewed may blow all of that out of the water and be far better. For that reason, stay impartial until you have made the final decision after discussing it with everyone on the panel.

When conducting a panel interview, you should ensure that those on the panel come from different backgrounds, have different viewpoints and different personalities. This will increase the chances of you choosing the right candidate and helps you to open up your mind to things you might not have seen for yourself. Obviously, those on the panel should be part of your recruitment agency but they should be experienced personnel. In some very rare cases, the client may be present, but this is far less common and is more likely to be from within the agency itself. There should be one person in charge of the panel, i.e. leading the discussion, with the others asking pre-selected questions.

Panel interviews are a good opportunity to see how candidates respond to different types of personalities and groups. However, that doesn't mean that one on one interviews aren't as valuable. In some cases, this is the best option because it saves time. Not all job roles require a large panel and if you feel that a one on one choice is sufficient, you can still ask the searching questions you need and come to a fair decision in the end.

## 8.2 How to Plan Interviews Correctly

Interview planning is a vital part of the process. If interviews aren't planned correctly, it increases the chances of a problem on the day, which could be time-consuming, time-wasting, and could completely derail the ultimate plan of making a hiring decision on the day.

First, you need to identify which type of interview is best for a specific role. You should invite your candidates by email or letter, but in some cases, you should call them and check they can attend too. The sooner you confirm numbers, the easier it will be to plan ahead and avoid changing the plan at the last minute.

If you are conducting a panel interview, ensure everyone has availability on that particular day and meet up beforehand to discuss questions, who is going to ask what and to give more information about the role overall.

After that, it comes down to specifics.

- Plan interviews spaced evenly apart throughout the day and be sure to leave around 20 minutes between interviews. This is especially important if you are conducting panel interviews as it gives everyone on the panel the chance to discuss their thoughts after one candidate has left and before another arrives. It also ensures that everyone has time for comfort breaks and remains focused on the series of interviews ahead.
- Before the first interview commences, spend half an hour catching up with the panel, checking that everyone remembers who is asking what and going through the candidates who are expected to arrive throughout the day. You should also present the job description to keep it fresh in everyone's minds.
- Copies of the job description, person specification and the CVs of those attending for interview should be given to the interview panel if you are indeed having a panel interview. If you are having a one on one interview, spend some time going over the CVs beforehand to refresh your own

memory. It's also a good idea to keep the job description handy, so you can refer back to it. Interview days can be very tiring and it's important to keep your mind focused on the task at hand.

- Double-check room bookings beforehand, to ensure that the meeting room isn't double-booked. Also check you have ordered catering, if necessary and that there is access to refreshments.

- Lay the interview room out in a way that isn't terrifying to the client. Having a long table with several people sitting there can be unnerving for a candidate and it may mean that their nerves get the better of them, therefore robbing you of seeing them in their best light. It's a better idea to have chairs arranged in a semi-circle and to avoid tables, which act as a barrier. If you're having a one on one interview, you could sit with two chairs facing one another and a small table to one side, so you can lean on it to make notes.

- Make sure you make the candidate feel comfortable. Offer them refreshments, smile, nod, encourage them and don't terrify the life out of them! Whilst this is a formal interview, you are trying to find the best candidate for the job and that means encouraging them to show their best side. Many candidates will freeze if they feel under undue pressure and that's only going to cause you to miss out in the end.

Once you have completed interviews for the candidates you want to see, it's time to think back and go through your notes, before arriving at a final decision on who you want to hire.

There are however three main approaches to interviews that you should be aware of. These will set the tone of the interview and allow you to keep your mind on what you're really looking for. They are:

- Behaviour
- Competencies
- Situations

By focusing on one or possibly two of the above types, you're able to streamline your approach to the specific role itself. This will help you to find the best candidate for the job. For instance, a role which relies upon personality rather than having a set type of qualification would mean focusing on behaviour, rather than asking leading questions about training.

Once you have made a decision on who to hire, you will need to inform the candidate themselves and of course, inform the client that you have successfully found the perfect candidate for their vacancy.

## 8.3 The Importance of Background Checks

Before a job offer can be made, there are often background checks which need to be completed. Until the results of these checks have returned satisfactorily, a formal offer letter cannot be sent. You can, however, send a provisional letter which states the checks which need to be performed and that the job role has been provisionally offered, pending test results.

The most important thing to check before offering a role to anyone is to ensure that they have the legal right to work in the UK and that they have up to date, accurate and legitimate paperwork to back this up. Of course, this should have been checked at the receiving CV stage, but it's something you will need to recheck before offering a role to a candidate.

There are also background checks which are mandatory depending upon the job role you're applying for. The law in the UK demands on a CRB check (criminal records check) for any individual who is potentially going to work with children or in health. The results of this check will inform your decision on whether to move ahead with the hire or whether to, unfortunately, cancel it and choose another candidate.

Of course, you need to inform the candidate of any checks which are being conducted in their name and you need to obtain their consent. If they refuse consent, meaning you cannot conduct the check, the provisional job offer will need to be revoked. Refusing consent for a background check should cause suspicion and lead you to think that perhaps they're not telling you everything. In this case, they're not the right candidate for the job.

The main background checks that may need to be performed, depending upon the job role and the preferences of the client themselves are:

- **Credit check** - This type of background check isn't common but if a job role is going to involve the candidate having a large amount of financial responsibility, this type of check may become necessary. In this case, a credit check will give you information on their credit history and therefore their financial reliability and responsibility level, but it will not reveal their credit score.
- **Health screening** - Some job roles require a health check to be conducted however this should only be done if there is a legal requirement to do so and not simply at will. For instance, vision checks may need to be carried out for a role which involves driving long distance or working with heavy machinery.
- **Right to work check** - You should check that the candidate has the right paperwork to allow them to work legally in the UK and ensure that you have copies of these papers on file. Anything which you're not sure of should be flagged up and doubled checked. There are severe repercussions for hiring illegal workers, and in this case, ignorance of the situation will not be a line of defence.

- **References** - You may need to obtain references from previous employers to form part of the screening process before an offer is made. This isn't always the case, as these are sometimes asked for prior to the interview. However, if you need to ask for references, you should obtain two or three referees from the candidate and inform them that you will be getting in touch with them prior to a final offer letter being sent out and signed.

Ensuring that you have all background checks completed and satisfactorily signed off before offering the position formally means that you're cutting down the chances of an incorrect hire being made. This increases the chances of your client's satisfaction with your final choice and of course, means that you're more likely to be considered for their staffing needs in the future.

# Chapter 9:

## Creating the Perfect Client Strategy

**Chapter Aims:**

- An overview of successful client acquisition
- Understanding how to choose the right clients for your agency
- An overview of common pitfalls to avoid when acquiring clients
- How to find the best clients for your agency to work with

Once one cycle of the recruitment process is complete, you will no doubt be moving on to the next one. As your agency grows, or if you're working for a large agency, you may have several cycles working simultaneously, but as one cycle ends, you will certainly be looking for a client to work with on the next one.

Not every client will require a long-term working arrangement with your agency. It may be that once their current vacancy is successfully filled, they don't have any other vacancies for a few years. That means if you focus on your existing clients too much and don't place as much energy on acquiring new clients, you're going to run out of business pretty quickly. You, therefore, need to focus your mind on looking after your existing clients but also always being on the lookout for new ones to add to your business repertoire.

There are also a growing number of new recruitment agencies popping up all the time and it's natural for clients to switch between them as their needs twist and change. That means you're going to lose the odd client and whilst you should never become compliant and simply accept this fact, you should make peace with it as an inevitability on some level.

All of this means that you need to have a careful client acquisition strategy in place, just as you have a candidate acquisition strategy too.

## 9.1 The Importance of Proper Planning

When putting together your client acquisition strategy and indeed, when looking to improve the strategy you already have, you need to ensure that you plan everything out carefully. By planning, you have less chance of following a potential client lead which takes you towards a dead end and therefore wasting time which could lead towards a more successful working connection.

It's always going to be a possibility that you communicate with a potential client for a week or maybe even more and they drag their heels on making a decision. In the end, they come back with a negative. It's frustrating, but it is part and parcel of the acquisition process from time to time. By planning properly, you reduce the chances of this happening, although you can't cut it out completely.

The first thing you need to do is think carefully about your objective and the type of client that you're trying to capture. Do you want to achieve a high number of clients or are you looking for a specific type, e.g. a specialism?

You should also think carefully about where your clients are located. Geography is important in the grand scale of things because it makes communication less effective if time zones are involved. However, with proper planning, this doesn't have to be a major barrier towards success. A client who is far away from you may also prove difficult when sourcing the right candidates, however, this could also include an element of remote working, which opens up the number of candidates you can acquire and target towards these specific roles.

Ensuring that you know as much about the type of client you want to attract as possible will make the process far easier and that means thinking about the types of niches, you're interested in. If you're happy to go far-ranging, e.g. be a 'jack of all trades' that is going to give you a greater scope for success but the fees you can charge may be significantly lower than if you work within a specialised niche.

Again, it's something to consider and plan carefully.

## 9.2 Tips to Create a Strong Client Strategy

Having the right strategy will ensure that you develop a base of high-quality clients who will ensure your recruitment agency goes from strength to strength. Spending time chasing clients who lead to dead ends means that you could have spent that time communicating with a client who turns out to be encouraging and provides you with a steady supply of recruiting over the coming months or years.

To help you create a strong client strategy, be sure to follow these tips:

• Ensure that the clients you approach are in line with your overall long-term business plan. Do you prefer to work with small business or is your plan to expand into larger businesses? Make sure that you're making headway into your long-term plan with every client you approach.

- Opt for clients you know will work with you, rather than limiting yourself too much - It might be that you want to work for the big organisations, but if you're just starting out, it might be that you need to focus on the clients who are willing to work with you for a while and build it up from there.
- Sit down and design the ideal client profile. By knowing what you're looking for, you'll find it easier to target your search accordingly. This means thinking about location, performance, business culture, and their future goals.
- Look over your client list every so often and identify any improvements you can make to your strategy. By regularly reviewing your performance you can ensure that you're not missing any vital steps that could help you to attract higher quality clients. Refer back to our element on KPIs for more information on this.
- Can you also choose to work with specific niches which have low demand but high value? This is something you could add as a USP and will help you to attract the boutique level service which demand higher fees in your favour.
- Do you need to increase your staffing levels? If this is something you can do, e.g. if you're the manager, you may need to think about increasing your staffing levels and having certain staff members who specialise in certain areas. This will help you to provide a bespoke service to specific

clients who request details that you're currently not catering for.

- Check-in with your clients regularly and ask for feedback. Be sure that any comments they give you, you work on them and don't push them to one side. By showing that you're willing to improve on any elements you're currently offering to them, your clients will value your services far more.

- Whilst you should be highly prepared, being too prepared can leave you sounding robotic when you're communicating with a client. You need to try and build up a rapport, albeit a professional one. This means that whilst you should have as much knowledge at your disposal as possible, you still need to sound natural and approachable. This is more likely to help you acquire new clients, as opposed to a service that is 'overly shiny'.

## 9.3 How to Sidestep Common Pitfalls

There are certain mistakes that new recruitment agencies make time and time again and these mistakes adversely affect their ability to acquire new clients and therefore, grow their business.

To help you avoid these pitfalls, read the list below.

- Be sure that you're valuing your clients properly - If you simply base your valuation of a client on their revenue alone, you're not measuring accurately. There are many other elements that can affect their value, and therefore, their value to your business. Look at growth, future aims, and any developments in the pipeline too. When calculating value in terms of revenue, but sure to also think about the costs they payout every month and take that into account in the final figure.

- Focus on clients who will give you repeat business, rather than one-time business - Whilst niche clients will pay more, they are more likely to be one-time affairs. However, the lower-paying clients are more likely to use your service on a continual basis, and therefore being more valuable to you over time.

- Treat your clients as people and not a number - By approaching a client with pound signs in your eyes, you're not treating them in a personalised way. It's important to treat your clients and your candidates as human beings and look to meet their needs on that level. If you can do that, you're more likely to interact with them to a higher quality, give them what they want, and therefore ensure they come back to you in the future.

- Talking too much - Make sure that you allow the client the time to speak and that you don't simply talk them to the point where they become frustrated and lose interest. Your sales approach should be a two-way street.

- Do your research first - Never call a potential client that you know little about. It comes over as totally unprofessional and unorganised. Find out as much as you can about the client before you make the call and drop information into the call here and there, without it sounding like you're repeating their own facts back to them.

- Don't make false promises - At the start, it can be easy to promise the moon and the stars in order to successfully secure business, but you're quickly going to lose business and credibility if you can't deliver what you promise. Make sure that you manage expectations carefully.

## 9.4 Dealing with The Sensitive Subjects

At some stage during the client acquisition stage, you're going to have to talk about the sensitive subjects that nobody enjoys - budget and payment.

At the end of the day, a recruitment agency is a business and whilst you don't charge your candidates a fee, you do charge your client a fee. This needs to be fair and competitive, but you shouldn't under or oversell yourself in terms of what you charge.

The best approach is to discuss your pricing framework and explain the process, rather than telling them how much your services are going to cost. This eases the embarrassment on both sides and opens up a more positive dialogue. The best times to discuss this subject are either at the beginning of the sales pitch, so the client can decide whether your services are within their budget, or just before they make a decision. At this point, the client is already half-sold and interested so it's more likely that they're going to accept your pricing structure than refuse it. It's worth remembering however that they may need to get authorisation from a decision-maker before coming back to you with a final yes or no, so don't be disheartened if you don't get an answer immediately.

Keep your pricing as easy to follow and understand as possible and make sure that the client knows what they're getting for the price. Keep it transparent and offer reviews and testimonials from other happy clients if they still seem like they can't quite decide whether to go ahead or not.

# Conclusion

The recruitment industry in the UK is ever-growing and that means you need to be one step ahead of the competition at all times if you want your agency to not only thrive but to grow and be successful.

Working as a recruitment consultant is an extremely rewarding role. You are helping candidates to make changes to their working lives which could lead them towards achieving their full potential and being far more satisfied with the work they do. You're also helping clients to fulfill their staffing needs and therefore, having a helping hand in their future success.

There is much to learn in this industry and there are always rules and regulations which are being implemented and changed. It's vital that you stay ahead of the game when it comes to new regulations and legislation, and that you cover all bases to ensure that you're not making an accidental mistake which could have major ramifications on the future of your agency.

Learning to acquire and manage clients and candidates in the right way will lead your agency towards a wealth of repeat business over the coming years. However, always remember that the competition is fierce and there is always a new agency not too far behind you.

There is no room for complacency in the recruitment business, but it's certainly a career choice that will bring you great joy and satisfaction too.

# A Short message from the Author:

Hey, are you enjoying the book? I'd love to hear your thoughts!

Many readers do not know how hard reviews are to come by, and how much they help an author.

I would be incredibly thankful if you could take just 60 seconds to write a brief review on Amazon, even if it's just a few sentences!

You can leave a review under the Orders page, at the links below.

https://www.amazon.com/your-account
https://www.amazon.co.uk/your-account

Thank you for taking the time to share your thoughts!

Printed in Great Britain
by Amazon

39348982R00091